Jokes Not To Tell Your Teacher

ANSWERS TO PUZZLES ON PAGES 92-96

HOWARD — A SIX YEAR OLD PIANO-PLAYING BUDGIE, AND DIPLOMATIST.*

* SEE OTHER BOOKS IN THIS STUPENDOUS SERIES...
  ID

JOKES NOT TO TELL YOUR PARENTS

JOKES NOT TO TELL YOUR GRAN

JOKES NOT TO TELL YOUR FRIENDS.

Jokes Not To Tell Your Teacher

Gill Brown

Illustrated by David Mostyn

RED FOX

A Red Fox Book

Published by Random Century Children's Books
20 Vauxhall Bridge Road, London SW1V 2SA
A division of the Random Century Group

London Melbourne Sydney Auckland
Johannesburg and agencies throughout the world

Red Fox edition 1991

Text © Gill Brown 1991
Illustrations © Oxford Graphics 1991

The right of Gill Brown and David Mostyn to be identified as the
author and illustrator of this work respectively has been asserted by
them in accordance with the Copyright, Designs and Patents Act, 1988.

This book is sold subject to the condition that it shall not, by way of trade
or otherwise, be lent, resold, hired out, or otherwise circulated without
the publisher's prior consent in any form of binding or cover other than
that in which it is published and without a similar condition including this
condition being imposed on the subsequent purchaser.

Set in Century Oldstyle
Typeset by Getset (BTS) Ltd
Printed and bound in Great Britain by
Cox & Wyman Ltd, Reading, Berks.

ISBN 0 09 974940 8

KONTENTS
see me after school!
I ALWAYS KNEW THIS BOOK WAS IFFY!
SEE! I KNEW IT WAS AN EAGLE!
TERENCE – A WET, SOPPY SNAKE

ALSO BY DAVID MOSTYN AND PUBLISHED
BY RED FOX, "HOW TO DRAW CRAZY CARTOONS."

— DEDICATION —

TO ALL KIDS WHO ENJOY A GOOD WACKY JOKE

How many times can you take 3 away from 3,333?
Only once. After that you're taking it away from 3,330 and so on.

Who invented fractions?
Henry ⅛.

TEACHER: What is a centimetre?
STINKER: An insect with a hundred legs.

How do Russian schoolchildren dress in winter?
Quickly!

GEOGRAPHY TEACHER: What can anyone tell me about Chile?
ANDREW: It's the coldest place on earth.

'Mum, can I have a new pair of plimsolls for gym, please?'
'I don't see why Jim can't buy his own.'

FREDDIE: This egg is bad.
DINNER LADY: Don't blame me. I only laid the table.

CRAZY CLASSROOM

How many things can you find wrong with this crazy classroom?

HOW MANY?

If you really want to get your teacher worried, try asking him or her these very silly questions!
How many . . .
1. Sides has a circle?
2. Legs has a football player?
3. Lines has a railway track?
4. Days in the year are your birthday?
5. Fingers have two sets of twins?
6. Teachers are there in your school?
7. Hairs are there on your head?
8. Grannies does anyone have (originally)?
9. Hours are there in a day?
10. Players are there in a game of tennis (singles)?

LYNNE: I know how we can find out how old our teacher is.
WYNNE: How?
LYNNE: By taking her knickers off.
WYNNE: How will that tell us her age?
LYNNE: Well the label in my knickers says '7 to 9'.

TEACHER: Who can tell me how an Eskimo builds his house?
TRACEY: 'E glues it together.

HEADMASTER: I'm afraid I can't start your car for you, Mr Leading, because the battery is flat.
MR LEADING: Oh dear. What shape should it be?

Knock, knock.
Who's there?
Andrew.
Andrew who?
Andrew a lovely picture in school today.

Books on the shelves of the school library:

Collecting Old Furniture by Anne Teak
A Book of Dinosaurs by Terry Dactil
The Sky at Night by I. C. Stars
Crossing the Sahara by Rhoda Camel
Jumping Off Beachy Head by Hugo First
The Gardening Handbook by Anita Lawn
Carpentry Made Simple by Andy Mann

WEATHER FORECAST

What is odd about this sentence?
No mists or frost, Simon.

Annie had just completed her first day at school.
'What did you learn?' asked her mother.
  'Not enough,' replied Annie. 'I've got to go back tomorrow.'

CALCULATOR CHAT

If you do not have a pocket calculator of your own, borrow a friend's. Divide 7734 by 10,000, turn the calculator upside down and see what it says to you!

SPELLING BEE

How good is your spelling? Which of these silly words is spelt correctly?

SILLLY, BANANANANANANA, SOSSIDGE

MARY: I thought you said there was a choice for dinner, but there's only shepherd's pie.
DINNER LADY: The choice is take it or leave it.

DINNER LADY: You should eat lots of carrots, they're good for your eyes.
FREDDIE: How do you know?
DINNER LADY: Well, you don't see many rabbits wearing glasses, do you?

DONALD: It said on our Doreen's school report that she was careless about her appearance.
RONALD: But your sister always looks very smart.
DONALD: Yes, but she only appears at school twice a month.

SUSIE: I wish I'd been born hundreds of years ago.
SALLY: Why?
SUSIE: There wouldn't have been as much history to learn.

Clarence was the school swot. The other children used to pick him up and swot flies with him.

IF I BOUGHT A HUNDRED CURRANT BUNS FOR £1, WHAT WOULD EACH BUN BE?
STALE, MISS.

I'LL JUST TAKE YOUR PULSE, KATE.
WHY? HAVEN'T YOU GOT ONE OF YOUR OWN?

? ? ? ? ?

You might have one of these at 11 o'clock in the morning. What is it?

STINKER: Mum, will you do my homework for me?
MOTHER: No. It wouldn't be right.
STINKER: Well, you could at least try.

TEACHER: Construct a sentence using the word 'unaware'.
DILBERT: 'Unaware' is what we put on under our shirts and trousers.

What exams did Santa Claus take?
Ho, ho, ho levels.

TEACHER: You missed school yesterday, didn't you, Freddie?
FREDDIE: No, sir, not one bit.

TEACHER: Order, order, please, children!
STINKER: Two hamburgers with French fries, please.

TEACHER: Who can tell me which month has twenty-eight days?
CLEVER CLARA: All of them do, Miss.

NORA: Why do you call your form mistress Miss Peach when her name is Smith?
NELLIE: Because she's got a heart of stone.

TEACHER: I despair of you, Sam. I don't see how it is possible to get so many things wrong in one day.
SAM: Well, I always get here early, Sir.

What comes right up to the school door but never goes in?
The path.

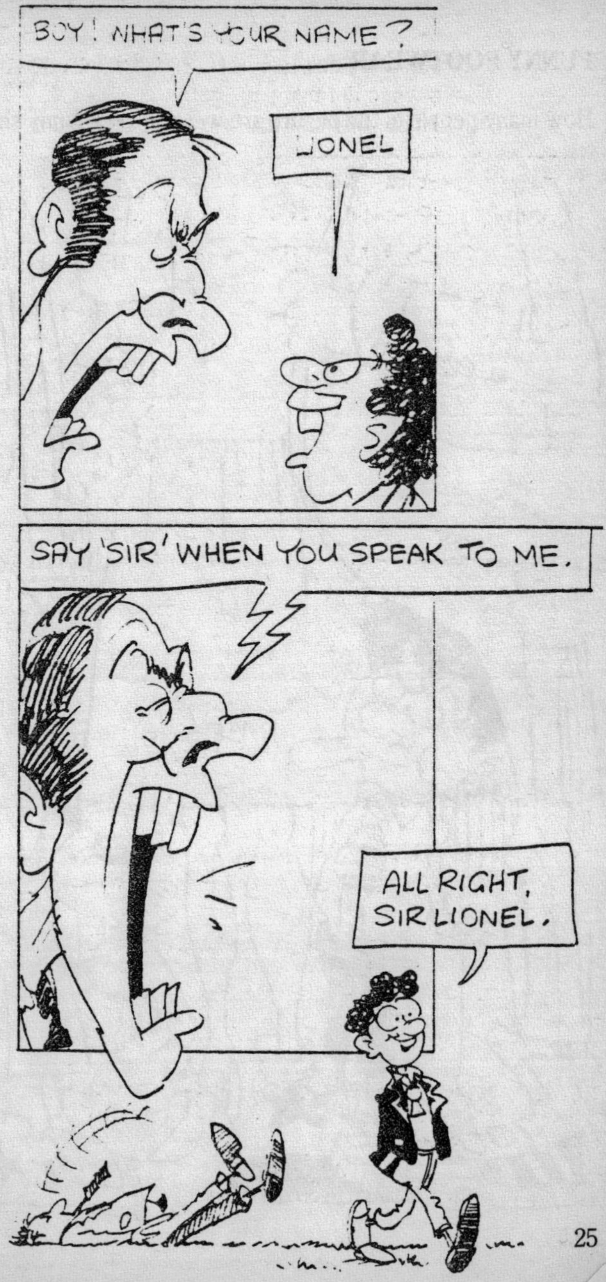

FUNNY FOOTWEAR

How many people in the picture are wearing very funny shoes?

CLASSROOM CONUNDRUM

When is a teacher two teachers?

FATHER: Your marks for history are not very good, Samantha.
SAMANTHA: That's because our teacher keeps asking me questions about things that happened before I was born.

MATHS TEACHER: If you add 53917 to 47891, divide the answer by 2 and then multiply it by 5, what do you get?
KATE: The wrong answer.

HISTORY TEACHER: What was the first thing Queen Victoria did on coming to the throne?
JACQUI: Sat down, Miss?

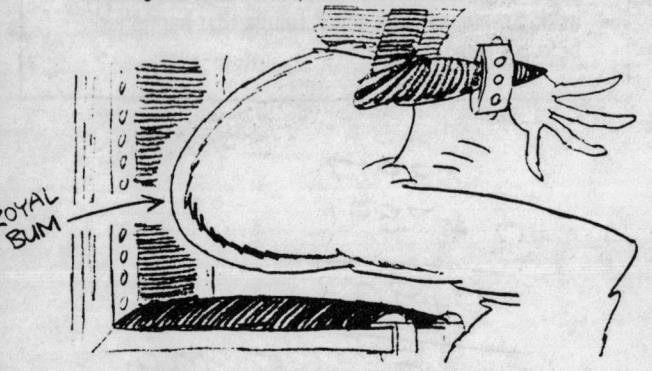

Why did the school move the chickens out of the playground?
So the pupils wouldn't overhear fowl language.

Why is a pencil the heaviest thing on your desk?
Because it's full of lead.

TEACHER: How old are you, Darren?
DARREN: I'm not old, Miss, I'm almost new.

Why did the headmaster stand on his head?
He was turning things over in his mind.

NEXT, PLEASE

What are the next three letters in the series?

J F M A M J J A S — — —

FINGER IT OUT

If you are clever, you can prove to your teacher that you, unlike everybody else, have *eleven* fingers! This is how you do it.

Start with your left hand and count up to five, then go to your right hand and count six, seven, eight, nine and ten. Then say, 'Let's try it backwards.' Count backwards on your right hand — ten, nine, eight, seven, six — then hold up your other hand and say 'And five makes eleven!'

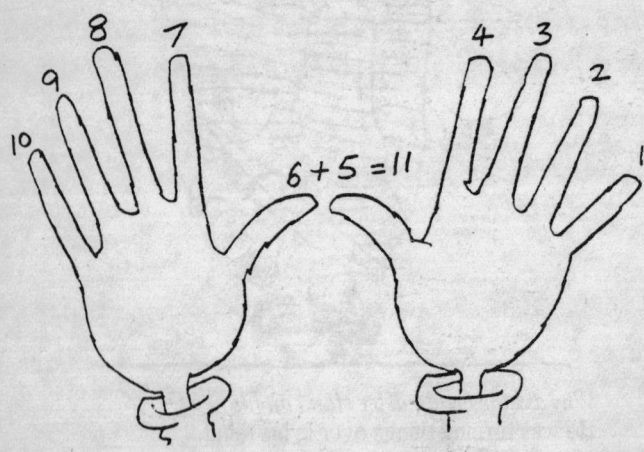

TEACHER: You've been fighting again, William, and this time you've lost your front teeth!
WILLIAM: No I haven't, Miss. They're in my coat pocket.

My spelling is

TEACHER: Who can tell me when the Forth Bridge was built?
STINKER: I can, Miss. It was after the third one fell down.

MATHS TEACHER: What is half of eight?
FREDDIE: Up and down, or across?
MATHS TEACHER: What do you mean?
FREDDIE: Well, up and down it's three, across it's nought.

ENGLISH TEACHER: Your handwriting is dreadful, Beatrice.
BEATRICE: I know, Miss. But if you could read it you'd know how good my spelling is.

really fantastic

Why is history the fruitiest lesson?
Because it's full of dates.

What's a Hindu?
Lays eggs.

TEACHER: Where is your pencil, Michael?
MICHAEL: I haven't got none, Sir.
TEACHER: I've told you before not to say that. It should be, 'I do not have a pencil, you do not have a pencil, he does not have a pencil. Do you understand?
MICHAEL: No, Sir. Why doesn't anyone have no pencils?

I'M LEAVING

TEACHER: Did you go to Italy for your summer holidays, Sharon?
SHARON: I don't know. My dad bought the tickets.

I'M COMING WITH YOU!

WILL THE PERSON WHO "BORROWED" THE CARETAKER'S LADDER RETURN IT IMMEDIATELY OR FURTHER STEPS WILL BE TAKEN.
WHAT A GAME.

REMIDEO ET YOUR AMICUS
REMIDEO WITH VOUS, TE SED
STAY ET SCRIBO LINES ALONE !!!

TEACHER: Why are you crying, Hattie?
HATTIE: Because Jenny's lost her tennis racket.
TEACHER: Why does that make *you* cry?
HATTIE: Because I was using it when she lost it.

GONE

* SEE PAGE 96 FOR ENGLISH VERSION AND REALLY LATIN !!!

39

What do you call a teacher with a seagull on his head?
Cliff.

When are school dinners noisy?
When they're bangers and mash.

— I HAVE GOOD NEWS, MUM
— DID YOU PASS YOUR EXAMS?
— WELL, NO — BUT I CAME TOP OF THE FAILURES.

TEACHER: Why are you late, Bill?
BILL: Well, sir, the sign outside in the road says, 'Go slow, children'!

DOES THAT MEAN TALKING TOO?

GO SLOW CHILDREN

CHEMISTRY CLASS

How many differences can you spot between these two pictures of a chaotic chemistry lesson?

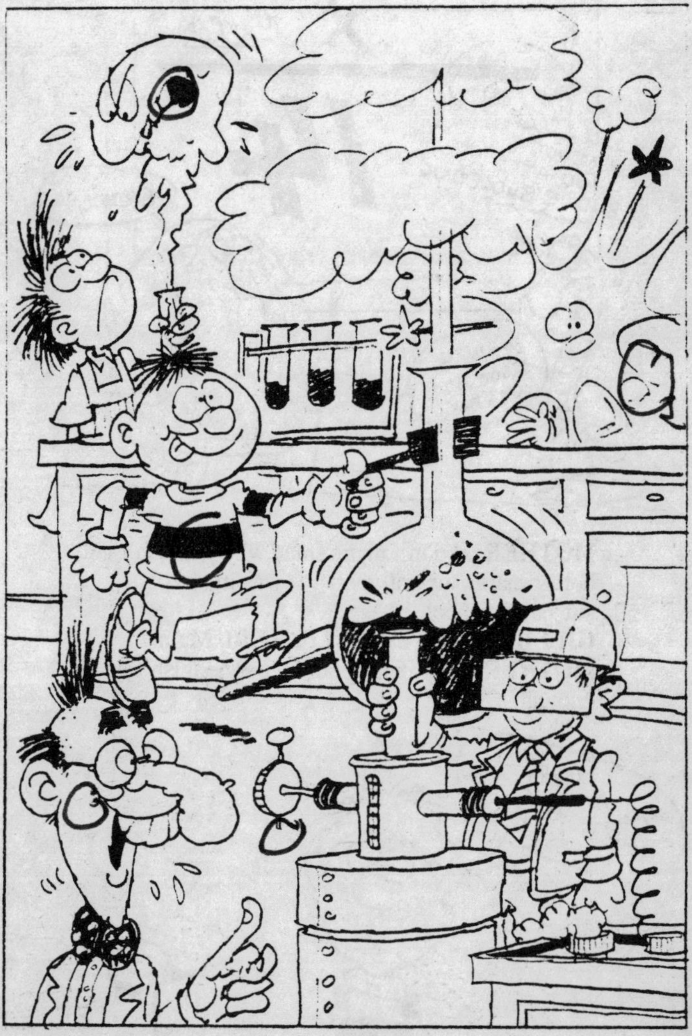

MOTHER: I don't understand why you don't get better marks for arithmetic. It was my best subject at school.
GILLIE: Well, I did get 7 out of 10, Mum.
MOTHER: Yes, Gillie, but 50 per cent isn't good enough.

SCHOOL BUS

Stinker was waiting for the bus to go to school. He waited for half an hour before a number of buses appeared. There were two buses in front of a bus, two buses behind a bus, and a bus in the middle. How many buses were there altogether?

The sports master was giving the class a first lesson in cricket.
 'Who can tell me how to hold the bat?' he asked.
 'By the wings, Sir?' replied Kate.

BATS ARE PROTECTED FROM BATS

HE'S BATS!

The chemistry teacher was explaining to her class how acids behaved. She took a £1 coin and dropped it into a beaker of acid.

'Do you think the acid will dissolve the coin?' she asked her class.

'No, Miss,' replied Freddie.

'That's right,' said the teacher. 'But how did you know the answer?'

'Well, Miss, you wouldn't have dropped it in the acid if you'd thought it would dissolve.'

ADORING MOTHER: Our Heather learned to play the piano in no time.
MUSIC MISTRESS: Yes. I've heard her playing like that, too.

FRENCH TEACHER: Who can tell me what *mal de mer* is?
DUMB DORA: Please, Miss, is it when you're saddle sore after riding a horse?

TEACHER: Now, children, you realise you cannot get eggs without hens.
CYRIL: My grandad can.
TEACHER: What do you mean, Cyril?
CYRIL: My grandad keeps ducks.

MATHS TEACHER: Jane, your figures are dreadful! That 1 looks like a 7.
JANE: It is a 7, Miss.
MATHS TEACHER: Then why does it look like a 1?

Pete arrived home from school with spots all over his face.

'Whatever's the matter?' asked his mother.

'I'm not sure,' replied Pete, 'but the maths teacher thinks I may have caught decimals.'

CLICK! CLICK!

Stinker's class is having its photograph taken. Which of the photographs is the one this photographer took?

51

"WHO CAN TELL ME WHAT A FORUM IS?"

"IT'S A TWO-UM PLUS A TWO-UM, SIR."

I COULD NEVER UNDERSTAND INDIAN

SUSIE: Miss Scales, the music teacher, said I had a heavenly voice.
SALLY: No she didn't. She said it was like nothing on earth!

I FEEL ONE OF MY HEADACHES COMING ON!

MOTHER: Did you get a good place in your exams, dear?
PARVINDA: Oh yes, Mum. I made sure I sat next to the school swot.

Why did 4C's classroom always have the lights on?
Because the pupils were the dimmest in the school.

TEACHER: Veronica! Why are you late for school?
VERONICA: Sorry, Miss. I overslept.
TEACHER: You don't mean to tell me you sleep at home as well?

AND WHILE SHE'S SLEEPING EATING ETC!

SCROTCH! SCROTCH!

WHAT WAS THAT?

Can you read the sentence below?

YY UR YY UB ICUR YY 4 ME

SLUB! SIT YREV YASE DEINDE*

*YEP! IT'S VERY EASY INDEED.

HOWARD – IN FACT ALL BUDGIES – ARE MULTI-LINGUAL IN ENGLISH, BUDGIE, RUSSIAN, RUBBISH AND FLEMISH.

ODD ONE OUT

Which of the muddled-up words is the odd one out?

```
SHIMTAMCATE
SHELING
STYRIHO
ROGEPHAGY
TEARCRYSE
```

DON'T BOTHER WITH THE ANSWER, P. 95 IT'S SHIMTAMCATE – ALL THE OTHERS ARE NAMES OF FILM STARLETS

WILL YOU LISTEN TO THAT! IT'S SO IMPRESSIVE!

NEWSFLASH: A large hole has been discovered in the playground of Littleton County School. Surveyors are looking into it.

ANSWER TO PAGE 96 OF "JOKES NOT TO TELL YOUR FRIENDS."

IT'S — "BULGE."

TEACHER: Who can tell me who Ivanhoe was?
STINKER: Er, was he a Russian gardener, Sir?

TEACHER, TO NEW GIRL: And what might your name be?
NEW GIRL: It might be Jane, but it isn't. She's my sister.

DAVE: Is this cottage pie?
MAVE: I think so. Why?
DAVE: Well fetch the nurse. I think I've just eaten a window.

IT'S OKAY! HE'S JUST GOT A LITTLE PANE!

Where's the best place to have the school sick room?
Next door to the canteen!

OH YEAH? RUMBLE!

Grace

HEAP BIG MEDICINE

Tell a friend you have magic powers, and can turn him into an Indian chief. Your friend is bound to ask, 'How?' at which point you say, 'See! The power is working already!'

WHEN MINNEHAHA GOT CHRISTANED SHE WAS MEANT TO BE CALLED MINNIE, BUT THE VICAR GOT THE GIGGLES!!

ODD (VERY ODD!) TEACHER OUT

Here are four pictures of Miss Fenella Flutington-Smythe, the music and drama teacher at Kate's school. Which of the pictures is different from all the others?

60

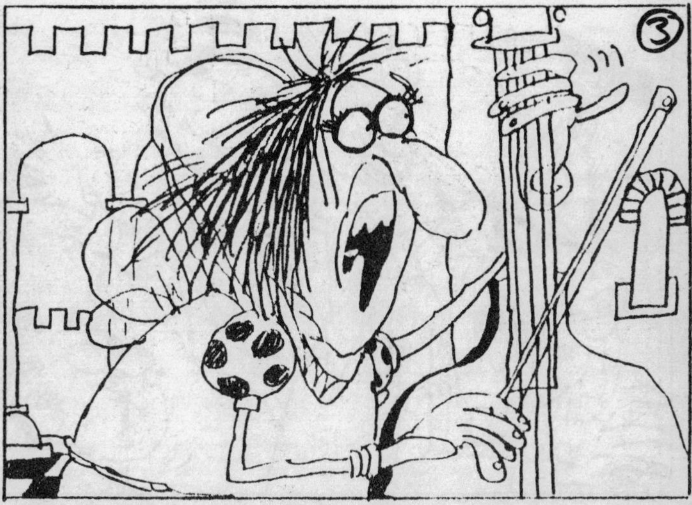
3

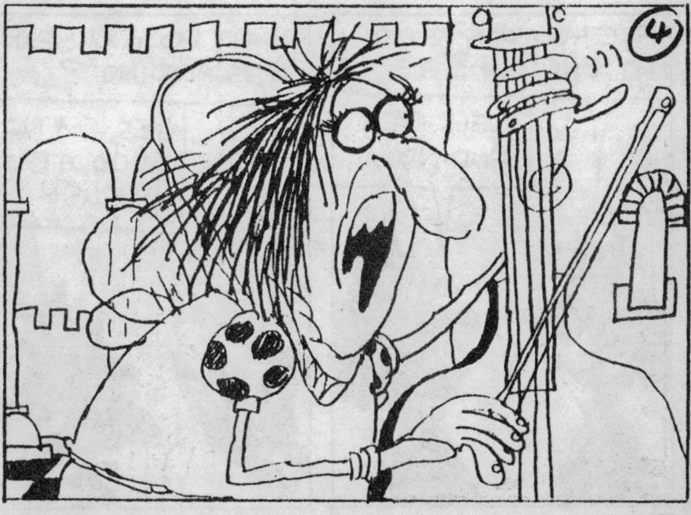
4

LENNY: I think our school is haunted.
BENNY: What do you mean?
LENNY: Well, our headmaster's always talking about the school spirit.

ARE YOU ANY GOOD AT ENGLISH?

WELL — YES AND NO.

WHAT DO YOU MEAN 'YES AND NO'?

YES, I'M NO GOOD AT ENGLISH.

TEACHER: Give me a sentence beginning with 'I'.
SARAH: I is . . .
TEACHER: No, Sarah. We don't say 'I is', we say 'I am'.
SARAH: OK. I am the letter of the alphabet that follows H.

Miss Scales took her class to a concert. Afterwards, little Sidney asked her why the musicians read books while they played.

'Oh,' laughed Miss Scales. 'They weren't reading books. They were looking at the score.'

'Really?' asked Sidney, amazed. 'Who won?'

AUNTY SUE: And how do you like going to school, Jenny?
JENNY: I don't mind going, and I like coming back, it's the bit in between I'm not too keen on.

Knock, knock.
Who's there?
Gladys.
Gladys who?
Gladys Friday.

GLADYS FRIDAY? I DON'T GET IT?

THAT SNAKE IS SO *WET*!

RIDDLE-ME-REE

What is it that no teacher wants, yet no teacher wants to lose?

'But, Mother, I don't want to go to school today. Please don't make me go!'

'But you must go, son. First of all, they are expecting you to go. And secondly, you're the headmaster.'

What's the difference between school tapioca and frogspawn?
Not a lot.

What happened to the bowl of daffodils in the maths classroom?
They grew square roots.

HISTORY TEACHER: Can you tell me what nationality Napoleon was?
NAUGHTY NED: Corsican!

I KNOW MY PASSPORT'S IN HERE SOMEWHERE!

What's worse than finding a caterpillar in your school salad?
Finding half a caterpillar.

I LIKE CATERPILLAR

What's yellow, stupid and often found on schoolboys' ties?
Thick school custard.

YUM YUM!

TEACHER: What was the Romans' greatest feat?
DOUGLAS: Learning Latin!

RIGHT – GET YOUR CHISELS OUT!

TEACHER: What do 2 and 9 add up to?
FREDDIE: 11.
TEACHER: Good.
FREDDIE: That wasn't good, it was perfect!

What do you call a school jacket that's on fire?
A blazer.

WHAT ON EARTH?

IF, IN THE SCHOOL CORRIDOR, YOU MET A PRECIPITATE PRECEPTOR, WHAT WOULD IT BE?

APRIL FOOL!

Here's how to give your teacher or your friends the horrors on April Fools' Day.

Buy some pipecleaners from a newsagent/tobacconist's, and cut and twist them into the shapes of spiders and caterpillars. (Remember spiders have eight legs!) Paint the spiders black, and the caterpillars green. The spiders can be left to lurk horribly in dark corners of the classroom, or hung suspended from a length of thread from a doorway or light fitting.

The caterpillars are very useful for slipping on to people's plates at lunch time, in the greens or the salad. If your teacher or friends don't notice them, put a hand on their arm, and, pretending to be horrified, say, 'I don't want to alarm you – but look! Ugggghhhh! Help!' When you've got them thoroughly alarmed, calmly pick up the offending 'creatures' and shout, 'April Fool!'

CRAZY ARITHMETIC

Look at these sums. They're quite crazy, aren't they? Or are they? Is there a way to make them make sense?

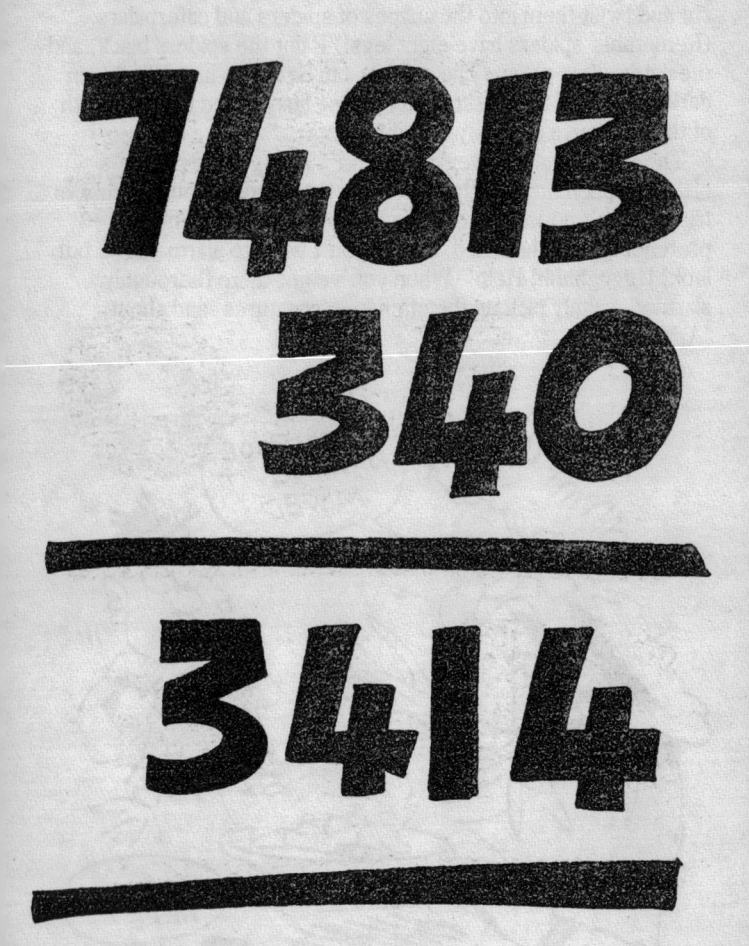

$$74813$$
$$340$$
$$\overline{3414}$$

$$734 + 340 = 3414$$

MOTHER: And did you enjoy your first day at school, Maria?
MARIA: First day? You mean I have to go there again?

FATHER: What's your favourite subject at school, son?
SUNIL: Gozinta.
FATHER: What do you mean, 'gozinta'?
SUNIL: You know, Dad, three gozinta six, four gozinta eight.

I WAS ALWAYS GOOD AT GOZINTA!

I THOUGHT GOZINTA WAS A DIRTY GREAT FILM STAR LIZARD!

If you have a referee in football, and an umpire in tennis, what do you have in bowls?
Porridge.

What does P.T. stand for?
Physical torture.

I'M AFRAID OUR TRACY IS ILL AND CAN'T COME TO SCHOOL TODAY.
I'M SORRY TO HEAR THAT. TO WHOM AM I SPEAKING?
THIS IS MY MOTHER.

Why did the teacher put corn in her shoes?
Because she had pigeon toes.

WHY DID FATTY BURNS COME FIRST IN THE 100 m SPRINT?
'COS HE HAD ATHLETE3 FOOT!

HISTORY TEACHER: What was King Arthur's court famous for?
STINKER: Its knight life, Miss.

GREAT PARTY ART BABY!

MAY I SPEAK TO YOUR MOTHER?
SHE AIN'T IN.

WAYNE, WHAT ABOUT YOUR GRAMMAR!
SHE AIN'T IN NEITHER, MISS.

ART CLASS

Join the dots to see what Freddie is drawing.

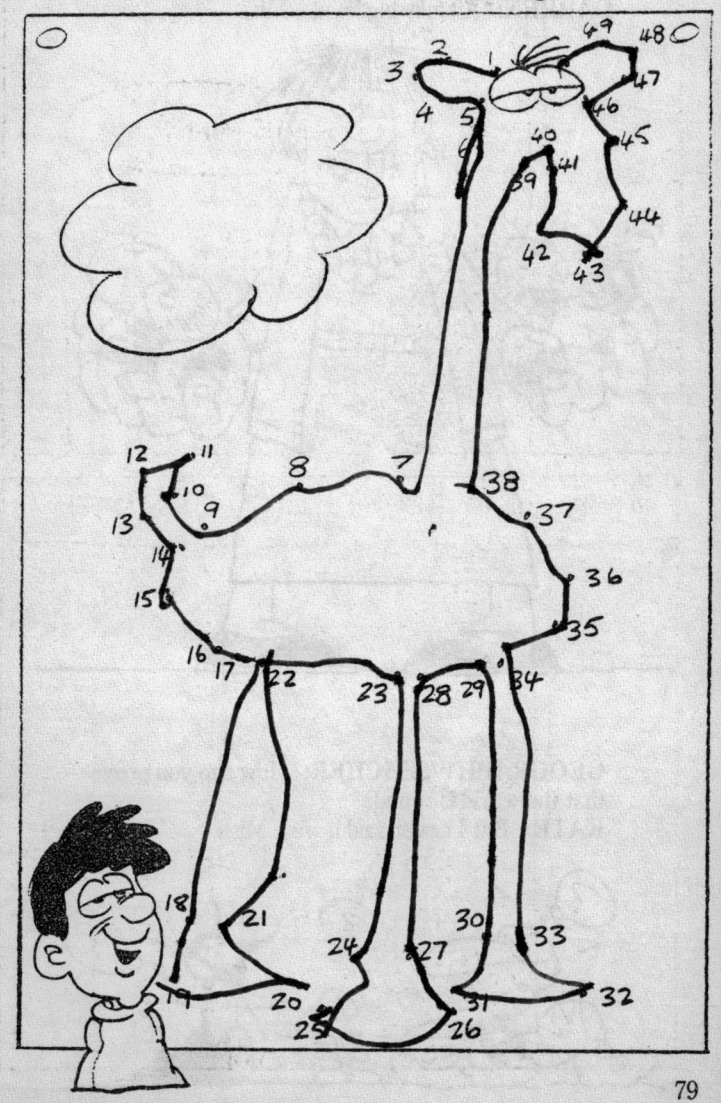

MATHS TEACHER: If I have four apples in my right hand, and five apples in my left hand, what have I got?
DARREN: Awfully big hands, Miss.

GEOGRAPHY TEACHER: How can you prove that the world is round?
KATE: But I never said it was, Miss.

NUMBER, PLEASE

Freddie's maths teacher was trying to catch him out. He said: 'If you add 5,555 to a certain whole number, the result will be more than if you multiply it by that number. What is the number?'

What should Freddie have answered?

Little Willie stamped into the house, threw his schoolbag on a chair, and announced, 'I'm not going there again!'

'Whatever's the matter, Willie?' asked his mother.

'Well, I can't read, and I can't write, and they won't let me talk, so what's the use?'

What's everyone's favourite saying at school?

I DON'T KNOW!

Lanky Larry was leaning back in his chair, with his feet stuck out in the aisle, noisily chewing gum.
'Larry!' roared out his teacher, 'take that chewing gum out of your mouth and put your feet in this instant!'

EVERY TIME I OPEN MY MOUTH SOME FOOL SPEAKS!

MOTHER: Why don't you like the new teacher?
CLARISSA: Because she told me to come and sit at the front for the present, and she never gave me a present.

Did you hear about the cross-eyed teacher?
He couldn't control his pupils.

HISTORY TEACHER: Where was the Magna Carta signed?
MAVIS: At the bottom, Miss.

HIGH JUMP

Say to a friend, 'I bet I can jump higher than our house.'

Your friend will think this is nonsense, and will take you on. You then take a little run, and do a little jump, and say, 'There! I told you I could jump higher than our house!'

Your friend will point out that you only jumped about 10 centimetres, at which you say, 'Ah, yes, but that's higher than our house, it can't jump at all!' Then run out of the way!

THESE ARE BURNING QUESTIONS!

MOTHER: Why have you been banned from cookery lessons?
KATE: I burnt something.
MOTHER: That doesn't sound too terrible. What did you burn?
KATE: The school kitchen.

MOTHER: WHY HAVE YOU BEEN BANNED FROM SCIENCE LESSONS?
JIM: BECAUSE I BLEW SOMETHING UP!
MOTHER: WHAT?

What has forty feet and sings?
The school choir.

CROSSED WIRES

Can you work out which Walkman belongs to which child?

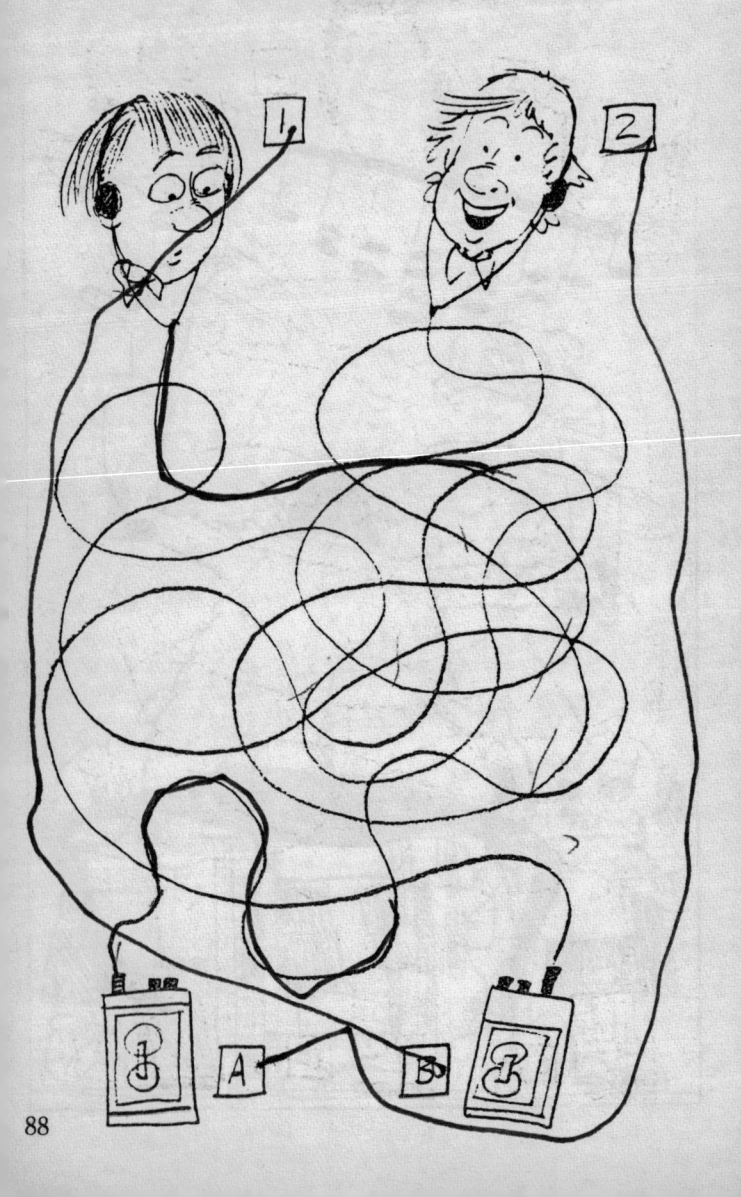

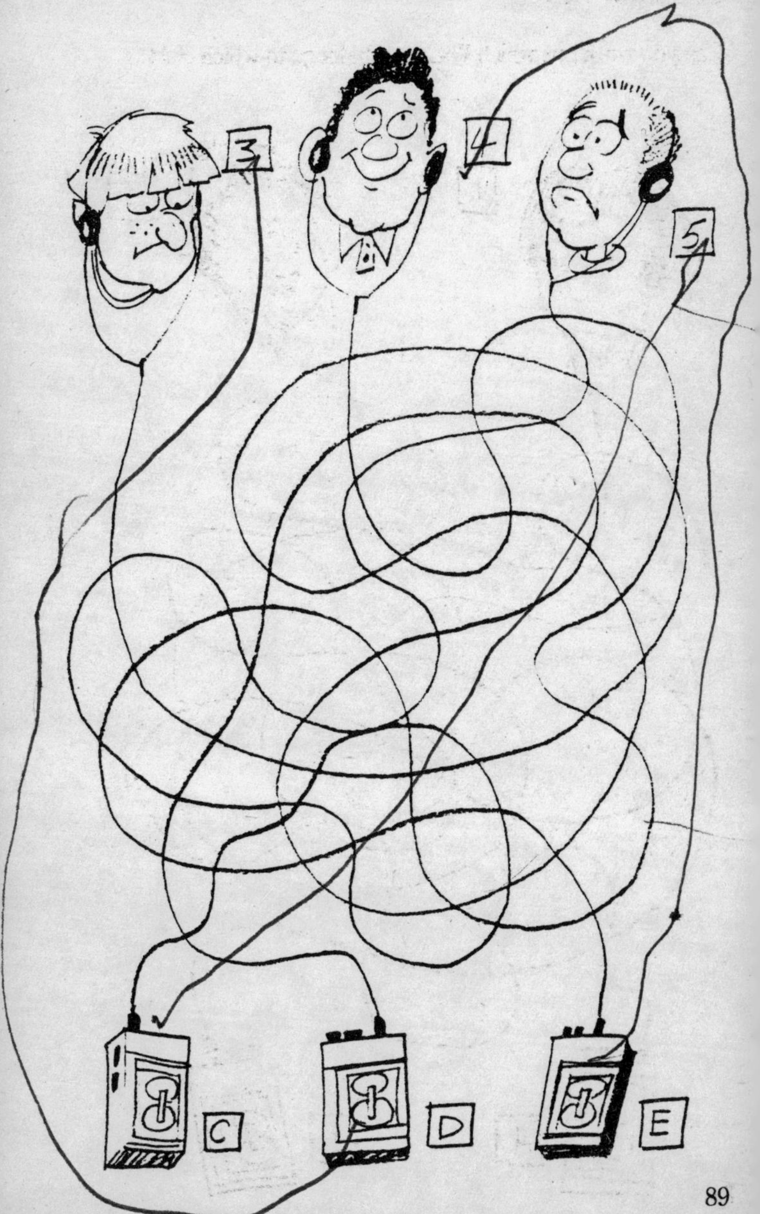
3
4
5
C
D
E

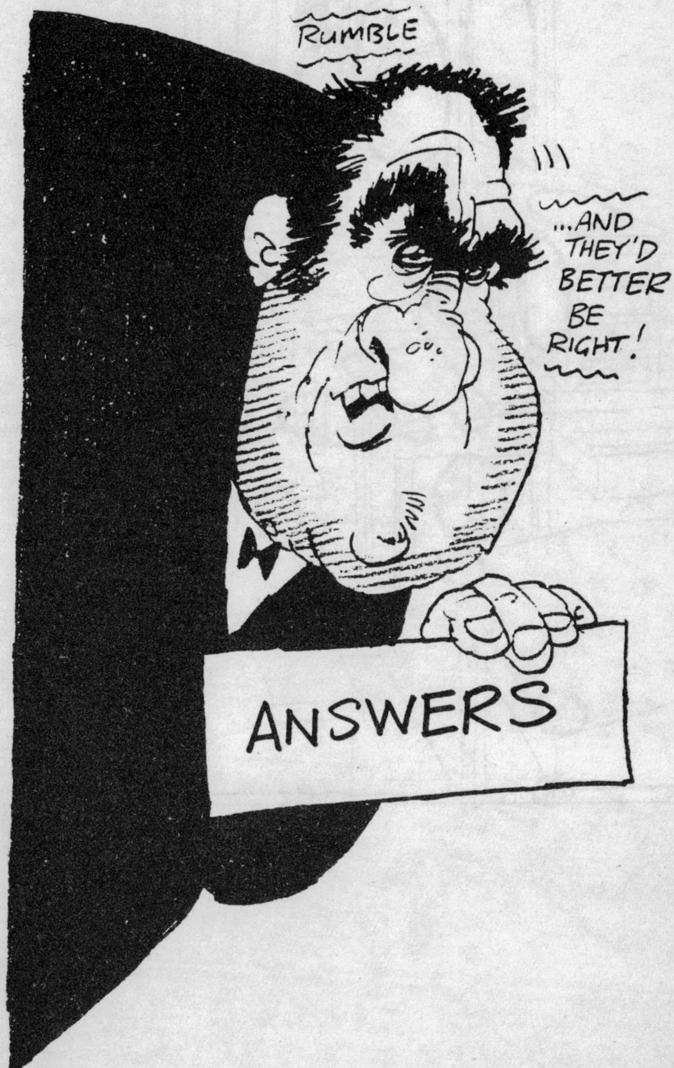
RUMBLE
...AND THEY'D BETTER BE RIGHT!
ANSWERS

P. 11 Crazy Classroom

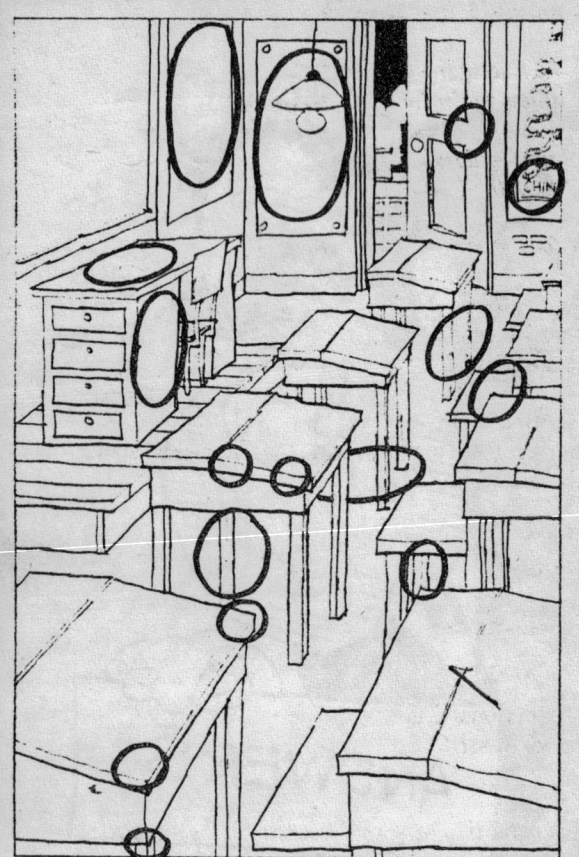

P. 12 How Many?
1. *Two – an outside and an inside.*
2. *Two.*
3. *Two on each set of tracks.*
4. *One – unless you're lucky, or the Queen!*
5. *Forty.*
6. *I don't know – do you?*
7. *About 100,000.*
8. *Two.*
9. *Twenty-four.*
10. *Two.*

P. 16 Weather Forecast
It reads the same backwards as forwards.

P. 17 Spelling Bee
None is! To make them a bit less silly, they should be spelt:
SILLY, BANANA, SAUSAGE.

P. 21 ? ? ? ? ?
It's a coffee break!

P. 26/7 Funny Footwear
Seven.

P. 28 Classroom Conundrum
When he's beside himself.

P. 32 Next, Please
O N D. They are the first letters of the names of the months.

P. 42 Chemistry Class

P. 45 School Bus
Three.

P. 50/1 Click! Click!
Picture number 3.

P. 54 What Was That?
Too wise you are, too wise you be; I see you are too wise for me.

P. 55 Odd One Out
TEARCRYSE, which makes SECRETARY. The others – MATHEMATICS, ENGLISH, HISTORY and GEOGRAPHY are all subjects.

P. 60 Odd (Very Odd!) Teacher Out
Picture number 2.

P. 65 Riddle-Me-Ree
A bald head.

P. 70 What on Earth?
A teacher in a hurry!

P. 72/3 Crazy Arithmetic
Look at the sums through a mirror.

P. 79 Art Class
Giraffe.

P. 81 Number, Please
1.

P. 88/9 Crossed Wires
1 – B
2 – A
3 – D
4 – E
5 – C

School motto: Laugh and your friends laugh with you, but you stay and write lines alone.

PROPER LATIN TRANSLATION.
———
RIDE ET TUI AMICI RIDENT TECUM SED MANES ET SCRIBIS VERSOS SOLUS!!
———
GOOD EH?

THE END

NOT A MOMENT TOO SOON

ACOUSTIC FEEDBACK

by

Vivian Capel

BERNARD BABANI (publishing) LTD
THE GRAMPIANS
SHEPHERDS BUSH ROAD
LONDON W6 7NF
ENGLAND

Please Note

Although every care has been taken with the production of this book to ensure that any projects, designs, modifications and/or programs etc. contained herewith, operate in a correct and safe manner and also that any components specified are normally available in Great Britain, the Publishers do not accept responsibility in any way for the failure, including fault in design, of any project, design, modification or program to work correctly, or to cause damage to any other equipment that it may be connected to or used in conjunction with, or in respect of any other damage or injury that may be so caused, nor do the Publishers accept responsibility in any way for the failure to obtain specified components.

Notice is also given that if equipment that is still under warranty is modified in any way or used or connected with home-built equipment then that warranty may be void.

© 1991 BERNARD BABANI (publishing) LTD
© 1991 Vivian Capel

First Published — August 1991

British Library Cataloguing in Publication Data
Capel, Vivian
 Acoustic feedback : how to avoid it.
 I. Title
 621.3892

ISBN 0 85934 255 7

Printed and Bound in Great Britain by Cox & Wyman Ltd, Reading

Contents

Page

Chapter 1
WHAT IS FEEDBACK? 1

Chapter 2
SOUND AND ACOUSTICS 5

Chapter 3
THE FEEDBACK PATH 27

Chapter 4
MICROPHONES AND FEEDBACK 35

Chapter 5
PEAKS AND NOTCHES 41

Chapter 6
FREQUENCY SHIFTERS 53

Chapter 7
GROUP MUSIC AND FEEDBACK 57

Chapter 8
HOW *NOT* TO CURE FEEDBACK 61

Chapter 9
DEALING WITH INSTABILITY 69

Chapter 10
BUILDING THE VARIABLE NOTCH FILTER ... 75

Chapter 11
USING THE NOTCH FILTER 87

Index 91

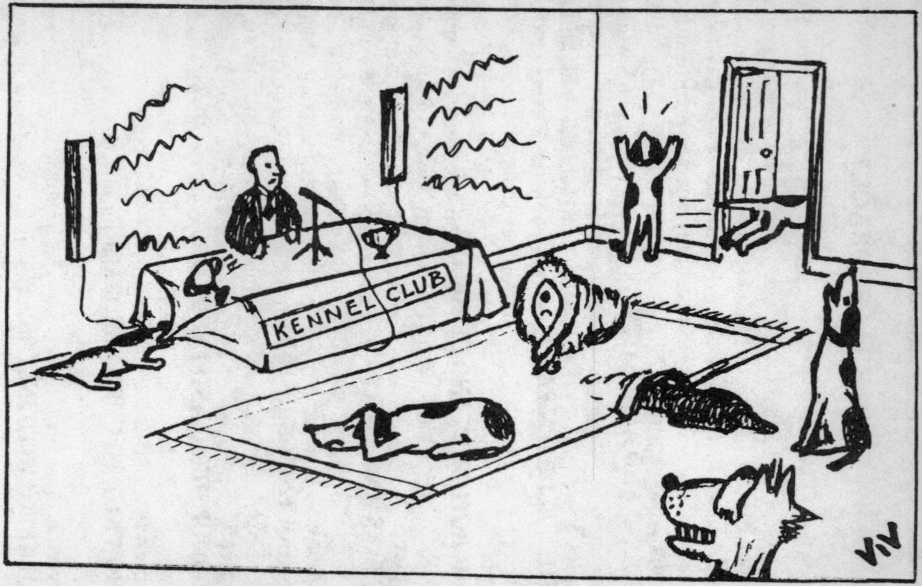
KENNEL CLUB

Chapter 1

WHAT IS FEEDBACK?

If you have ever tried to set up a sound amplifying system, whether in the local pub club-room, church hall, school assembly, or theatre; whether for a pop concert, play, or public meeting, you will have certainly encountered feedback.

You advanced the volume control, but before you got anywhere near a respectable level, howls, whines and whistles broke loose in a nerve racking crescendo. Hastily you turned it down, and the volume dropped to almost inaudibility. Cautiously you turned it up again, but then every spoken word was followed by a ringing effect that sounded as if the speaker was at the end of a long tunnel. You eased it back, but it was too quiet, a touch higher and once again it sounded as if you were at the end of the runway with Concord taking off. Out of the corner of your eye you saw a grim-faced secretary moving in your direction, but what could you do?

Familiar? Most operators of sound equipment have had some sort of experience such as this. With speakers that speak up and well into the microphone things aren't too bad, but the mumblers that think the microphone is just there for decoration, are just impossible to pick up. Yet you may visit another hall where there seems to be no problem; there is plenty of volume and no feedback. How do they do it? Is it your equipment at fault, or you, or what?

Don't lose heart, feedback is the number one bugbear of all p.a. systems, professionals get it as well as amateurs. It cannot be avoided, but it can be reduced to manageable levels — if you know how. That means knowing how it occurs, what affects it, and what inhibits it. We will look at all of these factors for there is no one simple answer. Firstly though let us answer the question: what is it?

Vicious Circles
Any random noise issuing from the loudspeakers is picked up by the microphone. It is passed through the amplifier, amplified, and fed to the loudspeakers which reproduce it louder

than before. Again it is picked up by the microphone and passes through the amplifier to be reproduced louder still from the loudspeakers. The microphone picks it up once more and the cycles continue with the volume increasing each time.

The result is the familiar howl. But why a howl, why not repetitions of the original sound? The original sound merely acted as a trigger to initiate oscillation in an unstable system. Any system that has amplification, and has positive coupling between its input and output is unstable, and when either the amplification or degree of coupling reaches a critical level, it will go into oscillation. The slightest disturbance will start it off.

In this case the coupling is the air mass between the microphone diaphragm and the loudspeaker cone. If there was no coupling there would be no feedback. So if microphone and loudspeaker are in different rooms and there was no air leak between them, no feedback would occur. This is why intercoms and baby alarms can be operated at high gain without any howl, unless they are in adjacent rooms with the doors open.

Feedback Rate

The feedback process happens a lot quicker than it takes to describe. Sound waves from the loudspeakers arrive back at the microphone at the speed of about 1,120 ft per second, so the feedback cycles occur at the rate of hundreds per second. That is why the sound is a continuous howl rather than a train of individual sounds.

Once started, the feedback arrives at the microphone in a continuous stream and so is not dependant on the distance between loudspeaker and microphone to determine the howl pitch or frequency. This is governed by the dominant resonance of the system, which is usually that of either the microphone diaphragm or loudspeaker cone. We will explore that aspect in a later chapter.

As each cycle of feedback is of greater amplitude than the previous one, it builds up rapidly. The ultimate limiting factor is the power rating of the amplifier. So, if the volume control setting is well over the critical point, feedback howl will occur at maximum amplifier power. Of recent years amplifier powers for public address have considerably increased due to the ease of obtaining high power from modern transistors. So, a full-blooded feedback howl from a modern high power amplifier is likely to be an awesome experience!

As the vital link is the air and the passage of sound waves through it, we need some knowledge of acoustics, which is the way sound behaves in an enclosed area such as an auditorium, in order to defeat feedback. We will consider this subject in the next chapter.

Chapter 2

SOUND AND ACOUSTICS

The feedback path between the loudspeakers and the microphone consists of sound waves travelling through air. The way they behave and how they are affected by the auditorium thus has an obvious and considerable effect on the nature and level of feedback. The study of sound, particularly in an enclosed area, is known as *acoustics* which is therefore one that has a special application to our subject. A knowledge of acoustics is also very useful in other related public-address matters. We will consider some of the basic principles that we need to know.

Sound Waves

The term *wave* although correct can be misleading. We usually think of waves as those seen at the seaside, vertical displacements of water consisting of ridges separated by troughs.

Sound waves, although behaving in a similar manner to sea waves or ripples on water in the way they are propagated, diffracted and reflected, are not vertical variations but consist of backwards-and-forwards motions of the air particles. These produce successive regions of compression and expansion or pressure differences, which spread outward from the source.

Air is a springy material, as anyone who has tried to operate a blocked air pump will have discovered, so the progress of sound waves can be illustrated by imagining a long coiled spring supported at its ends. A series of longitudinal impulses applied at one end travel along it as a train of compressions and expansions between the individual coils as shown in Figure 1.

Just as the coils of the spring do not travel from one end to the other but move backwards and forwards, so the air particles themselves do not move outward from the source, but each imparts oscillatory motion to the next.

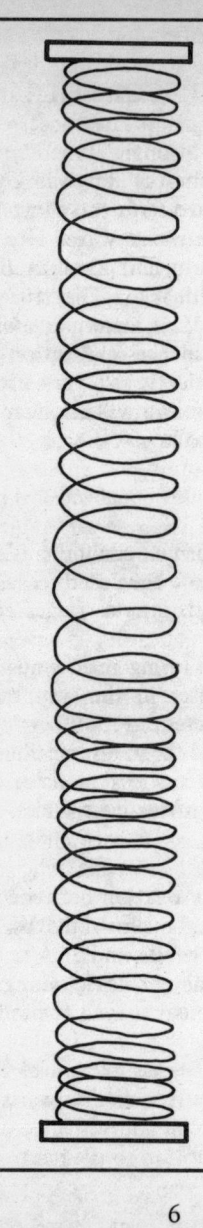

Fig. 1. A sound wave travels through air like a compression wave along a spring, producing travelling regions of high and low compression.

Wavelength and Frequency

Wavelength is obviously the distance from the crest of one wave to that of the next — or for that matter any part of a wave to the corresponding part of its successor. When a series of waves is travelling through a medium at a fixed speed we can count the number of waves that pass a given point in a given time. This we term the *frequency*. If the wavelength is short, there are many waves in a given area, and a large number pass the given point in the specified time. If though the wavelength is long, say twice as long as before, there will be only half as many waves in that area and only half the number will pass the point in the same time.

So there is a definite relationship between wavelength and frequency; as the wavelength gets shorter, the frequency increases proportionately. Sounds that are low in frequency are those produced in the bass register of musical instruments. These have long wavelengths. Those in the treble register are of high frequency and have short wavelengths.

Coming now to the technical terms used to describe these, frequency was once specified by the term *cycles-per-second* (c/s) and the multiple was the kilo; the *kilocycle-per-second* being a thousand c/s. This has now given way to the *hertz* (Hz) a less clumsy but also less obvious unit until you get used to it. The multiple is the *kilohertz* (kHz).

Wavelength has no unit other than physical length, usually expressed metrically. So we say that a certain sound frequency has a wavelength of so many metres, or if a high frequency, so many centimetres. It is often depicted by the Greek letter lambda (λ).

It should be noted that the relation between a particular frequency and its wavelength is governed by the speed of the wave through the medium. For sound this is 1,120 ft per second or 341 metres per second. This figure is for a temperature of 60°F (15.5°C); it increases by 2 ft per second for a temperature rise of each degree C. It is also affected by barometric pressure, but the effect is much less.

The concept of wavelength and frequency and their relationship is fundamental to all matters acoustic, so should

be thoroughly understood. If you are not too sure about it
re-read the foregoing paragraphs carefully.

Intensity and Pressure
Sound intensity is the amount of acoustic power passing
through a given area, usually 1 square metre. As with electrical power the unit is the watt. It is usually expressed as a
ratio of the faintest sound that can be heard — the hearing
threshold; at 1 kHz, this is 10^{-12} watts.

Sound intensity is used as a measure of total energy
generated by a source such as a piece of machinery which it
is required to silence, but it is not so often used for general
sound measurement, as is *pressure*.

We hear by reason of the pressure exerted on our eardrums from a sound wave, so the measurement of pressure
is one more directly related to our hearing. Likewise, most
microphones (though not all) are actuated by sound pressure
waves.

The sound pressure level is usually denoted by the letters
SPL, and if we compare it with electrical terms, it corresponds with the voltage in a circuit. SPL is the square root of
intensity.

Various units have been used to quantify pressure. These
are the bar, which is the atmospheric pressure at sea level;
the dyne/cm^2; the newton/m^2; and the pascal. The relation
between these is:

$$10 \text{ dyne/cm}^2 = 10 \, \mu\text{bar} = 1 \text{ newton/m}^2 = 1 \text{ pascal}$$

The pascal is the latest and the one now most commonly
used.

The Decibel
The decibel is often wrongly considered to be the unit of
sound level. It isn't, it is a unit that expresses a ratio
between two values. When applied to a sound pressure level
it denotes the ratio between that level and the threshold of
hearing. For pressure this is 20 μpascals.

Why use a ratio instead of some absolute unit for measurement? Because of the way our ears react to different sound pressures. They judge sound levels by their ratio to each other, and that perception is not linear. It is actually logarithmic. We have a sort of automatic volume control in our ears whereby the pivotal positions of the bones in our middle-ear region that convey vibrations from our ear drum to the inner ear sensor, the cochlea, change position with changes of volume. They are in the position for maximum transfer of energy with very quiet sounds, but in the minimum position for loud ones.

This remarkable design feature gives us a huge dynamic range, it allows us to hear the rustling of a leaf, yet also the roar of thunder without being deafened. The range from quietest to loudest SPL that we can hear is a million to one, and the sound intensity which is the square of that, is a million-million to one! No microphone yet made can handle a dynamic range such as that.

However, it somewhat complicates our sound measurements if we want them to relate to what we actually hear. Hence the decibel. When applied to sound pressure it strictly should have the letters SPL as a suffix, but usually they are dropped. The threshold having no ratio to itself is therefore 0 dB, the loudest sound we can hear without permanent hearing damage is 120 dB. Twice a particular level is an increase of 6 dB, four times is 12 dB, eight times is 18 dB, and so on. A difference of 1 dB is the smallest that can be detected.

Table of dB Ratios

dB	ratio	dB	ratio	dB	ratio	dB	ratio
0	1.0	2.5	1.334	10.0	3.162	50	316
0.1	1.012	3.0	1.413	11.0	3.55	60	1000
0.2	1.023	3.5	1.496	12.0	3.98	70	3162
0.3	1.035	4.0	1.585	13.0	4.47	80	10^4
0.4	1.047	4.5	1.679	14.0	5.01	90	3.16×10^4
0.5	1.059	5.0	1.778	15.0	5.62	100	10^5
0.6	1.072	6.0	1.995	16.0	6.31	110	3.16×10^5
0.8	1.096	7.0	2.239	18.0	7.94	120	10^6
1.5	1.189	8.0	2.512	20.0	10.0		
2.0	1.259	9.0	2.818	40.0	100.0		

Phase

Another important factor which affects the behaviour of a sound wave is its phase. As we have seen, the wave consists of alternate regions of high and low pressure. We have a compression region followed by a rarefied region. This can be visualized from the action of a loudspeaker cone as it moves backward and forward. The forward excursion compresses the air in front of it, while the backward movement rarefies it. It can be seen from this too, that while the front of the cone is producing a compression region, the back is producing a low-pressure one.

The two waves thereby produced are said to be *out-of-phase*. If two out-of-phase waves mix, the pressure peaks and troughs cancel each other and there is zero sound pressure. This happens at the rim of an unmounted loudspeaker, all wavelengths longer than the radius of the cone are cancelled but shorter wavelengths are unaffected. The tinny effect lacking in bass of an unmounted loudspeaker is well-known.

When two sound waves mix they may be in-phase and so reinforce each other, or they may be out-of-phase thereby cancelling. It is also possible that they may be only partly out-of-phase, with the compression region of one coming part way between the compression and rarefied regions of the other.

Phasing is thus not a black or white affair, there are grey areas too. For this reason it is likened to a circle and the sound waves are depicted as various radii of the circle. When two are exactly out-of-phase, the radii are in a straight line and opposite each other. They are thus said to be 180° out of phase. Other phase differences are also expressed in degrees of the circle. A quarter-cycle displacement is thus 90°, when the waves are said to be in *quadrature*.

Expressing phase in this way has a rather useful spin-off. If two equal in-phase waves reinforce and so produce double the pressure, and if two 180° out-of-phase waves produce zero, it follows that some in-between phase angle will produce a pressure that is between those extremes.

The resulting pressure (termed the *resultant*), and its phase relative to the others can be determined by a little geometry. All we have to do is to draw one line representing the first

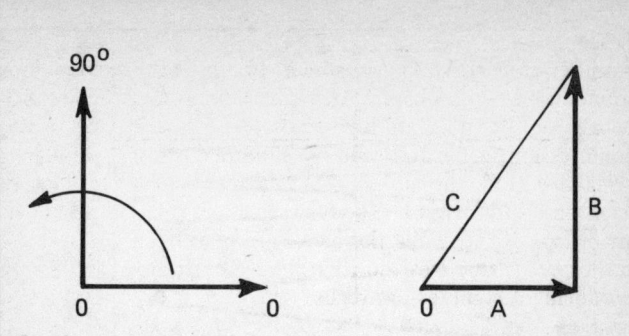

Fig. 2. Vectors. Signal amplitudes are indicated by line lengths and phase by angles. During a complete cycle the line rotates through 360°. If two signals A and B are drawn one from the end of the other, the phase angle and amplitude of the resultant is determined by joining line C.

wave and another representing the second, drawn from the end of the first. If the lines are to scale and the drawn angle the same as the phase difference, a third line drawn to complete the triangle gives the value of the resultant to the same scale and its angle (Fig. 2). Such lines are called *vectors*.

Interference

In a hall or auditorium where loudspeakers are operating, there are numerous reflected waves as well as those directly from the loudspeakers. Many of these combine at various points to produce either reinforcement or cancellation. This is termed *interference*. When two waves meet that have travelled paths of a different length from the same source, there are phase differences. But these are not constant, they vary with wavelength.

For example, a sound path difference of 6.75 inches is equal to the half wavelength of 1 kHz, so at any location with such a difference there is cancellation of 1 kHz, also at 3 kHz which is 1½ times the wavelength, at 5 kHz which is 2½ times, at 7 kHz which is 3½ times, and so on.

At 2 kHz which is a whole wavelength, there is reinforcement, also at 4 kHz which is twice the wavelength, 6 kHz

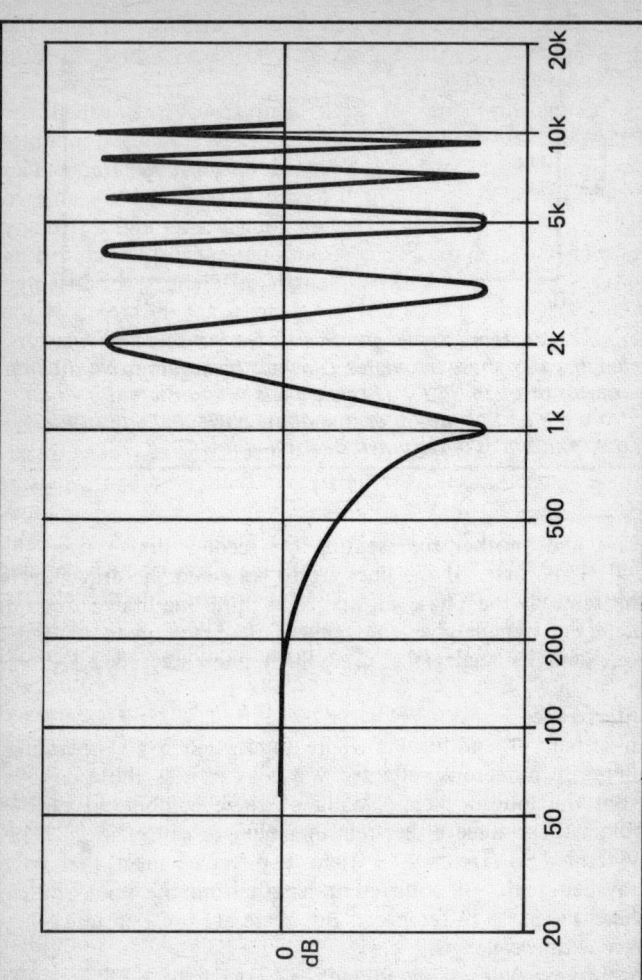

Fig. 3. Comb filter effect. With a sound path difference of 6.75 inches from two sources of equal amplitude, there is a fall-off to total cancellation at 1 kHz, followed by reinforcement at 2 kHz, further cancellation at 3 kHz and so on. Different sound path differences give different frequency points, but the pattern is the same. The result is chopping up of the higher speech frequencies with loss of intelligibility.

three times, and 8 kHz, continuing upward. From the cancellation at 1 kHz the sound level rises gradually toward the bass register (Fig. 3).

This violent series of peaks and troughs, is called the *comb-filter effect*, because the frequency response resembles the teeth of a comb. As noted before, the frequencies involved depend on the path length difference between two nearby loudspeakers or from one loudspeaker and a strongly reflected wave, and so varies from one seat in the auditorium to another. At other path-length differences the affected frequencies and comb-filter wavelengths are different. If the seat location is within a quadrant of four ceiling loudspeakers, the response is more complex, being the resultant of all four pressure waves.

The comb-filter effect can ruin intelligibility as its effects are worse at the higher frequencies that give clarity to speech. Ideally, the fewer loudspeakers radiating in the same area the better. This is one of the several reasons why rows of ceiling loudspeakers in a hall is one of the worst arrangements possible. The best is the LISCA (Line Source Ceiling Array), which radiates coherent sound free from any interference or comb-filter effects. It is fully described in the book BP292 *Public Address Loudspeaker Systems*, by the same author and publishers as this book.

Another area where a comb-filter effect can be encountered is near a microphone if there is a hard reflective surface such as a table top nearby. Sound from the source can reach the microphone directly and also via a longer path reflected from the surface. This is even more serious because it affects the whole audience not just sections, as does loudspeaker interference.

Propagation

A *point source* which is also termed a *monopole*, is one that radiates equally in all directions. The sound waves travel outward in the form of expanding concentric spheres. As the sphere expands, the energy at any point on the sphere decreases because it is spread over an increasing area. If we take a look at Figure 4, we see a segment of a sphere and at a distance from the point source d there is an area A. At twice the distance the area has increased four times, and at three

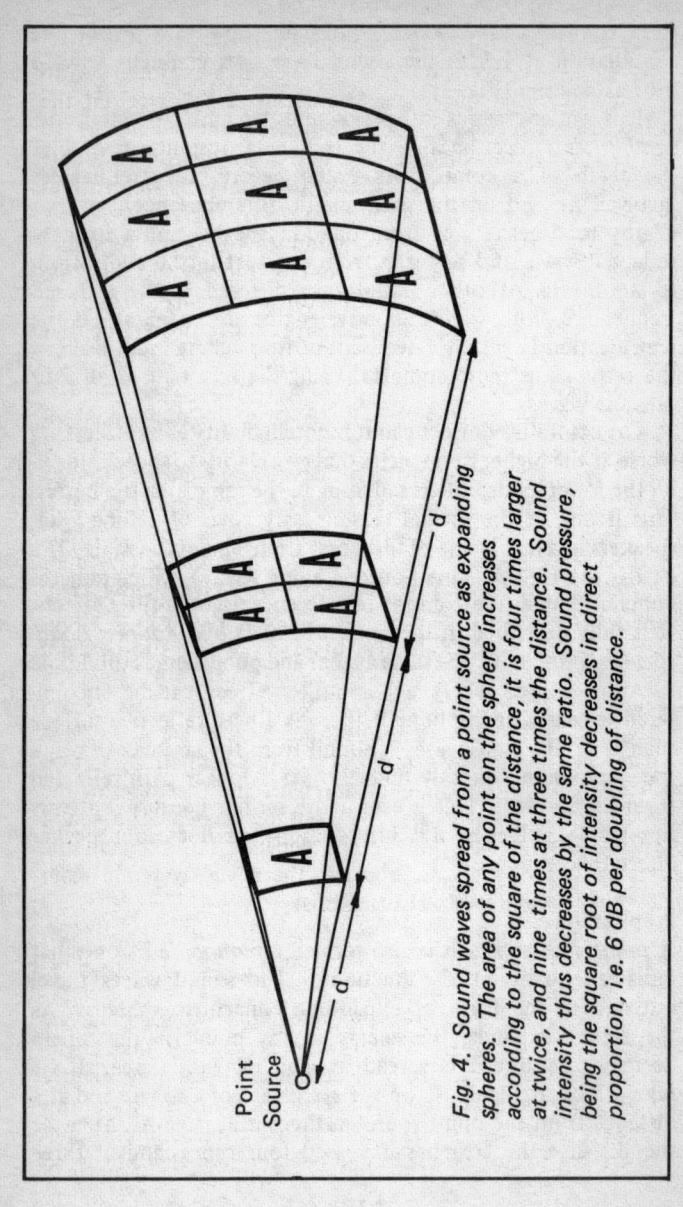

Fig. 4. Sound waves spread from a point source as expanding spheres. The area of any point on the sphere increases according to the square of the distance, it is four times larger at twice, and nine times at three times the distance. Sound intensity thus decreases by the same ratio. Sound pressure, being the square root of intensity decreases in direct proportion, i.e. 6 dB per doubling of distance.

times the distance it has increased nine times.

So the area obeys a square law, it increases in proportion to the square of the distance. From this it follows that the energy in each section A, must decrease by the same order, so obeying an inverse square law. It becomes a quarter at double the distance, a ninth at three times the distance, a sixteenth at four times the distance, and so on.

However, this applies to the sound wave power. As sound pressure is equal to the square root of the power, then the SPL decreases in *direct* proportion to the distance. Thus it is half or −6 dB at double the distance, and a quarter at four times the distance.

A loudspeaker in a sealed box is a monopole at all frequencies having wavelengths greater than the dimensions of the cabinet.

Attenuation is thus mainly due to spread-with-distance rather than distance itself. If prevented from spreading, such as in a heating duct or speaking tube, sound can travel long distances with little decrease. Loss which is due solely to air absorption is dependant on frequency. At 1 kHz, there is only a 2 dB drop over 1,000 ft. At 2 kHz, the drop is about 5 dB at 500 ft, while at 3 kHz there is a 10 dB drop at 500 ft. At 10 kHz the fall is 10 dB over 100 ft. In the speech frequency range and over the dimensions of most halls, it can be seen that loss due to air absorption is negligible.

The *dipole* or *doublet* has a figure-8 radiation pattern with two circular lobes, one at the back and the other at the front (Fig. 5). These are 180° out of phase. The sound pressure level at any given point depends not only on the distance from the source, but also the angle from the main axis. The formula for calculating it is:

$$SPL_2 = SPL_1 \cos a$$

in which SPL_1 is the on-axis sound pressure level, a is the angle of deviation, and SPL_2 is the sound pressure at that angle.

It is worth noting that while the levels drop only slightly just off axis, they drop rapidly thereafter for small deviations of angle. The half level is 60°. Most public-address loudspeakers are of the doublet type being in unsealed boxes, so

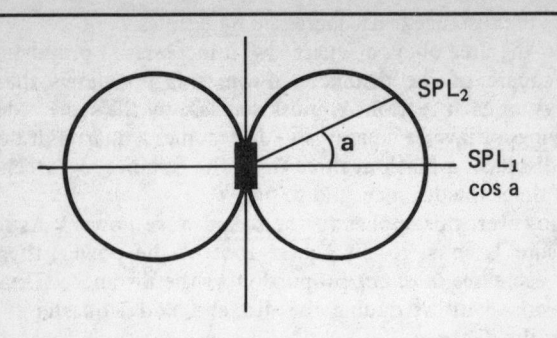

Fig. 5. Polar diagram of doublet. Off axis sound pressure level is equal to that on axis, times the cosine of the angle.

Table of SPL_2 Values

0°	1.0	25°	0.906	50°	0.647	75°	0.259
5°	0.996	30°	0.866	55°	0.537	80°	0.174
10°	0.985	35°	0.819	60°	0.500	85°	0.087
15°	0.966	40°	0.766	65°	0.423	90°	0
20°	0.940	45°	0.707	70°	0.340		

these angles are useful in determining coverage and feedback characteristics. As with the monopole, the pressure attenuation with distance is 6 dB for a doubling of distance.

A *line source* radiating sound through 360°, does so in the form of expanding concentric cylinders rather than spheres (Fig. 6). The propagation is restricted to the horizontal plane and so the attenuation is less than for a monopole or dipole. It is −3 dB for a doubling of distance which is −6 dB for quadrupling. It thus carries twice as far as a monopole or dipole.

The principle is used in the column loudspeaker which has a vertical array of drivers. However, it is not a true omnidirectional line source as the side and rear propagation is restricted. The polar pattern viewed from above is as shown in Figure 7.

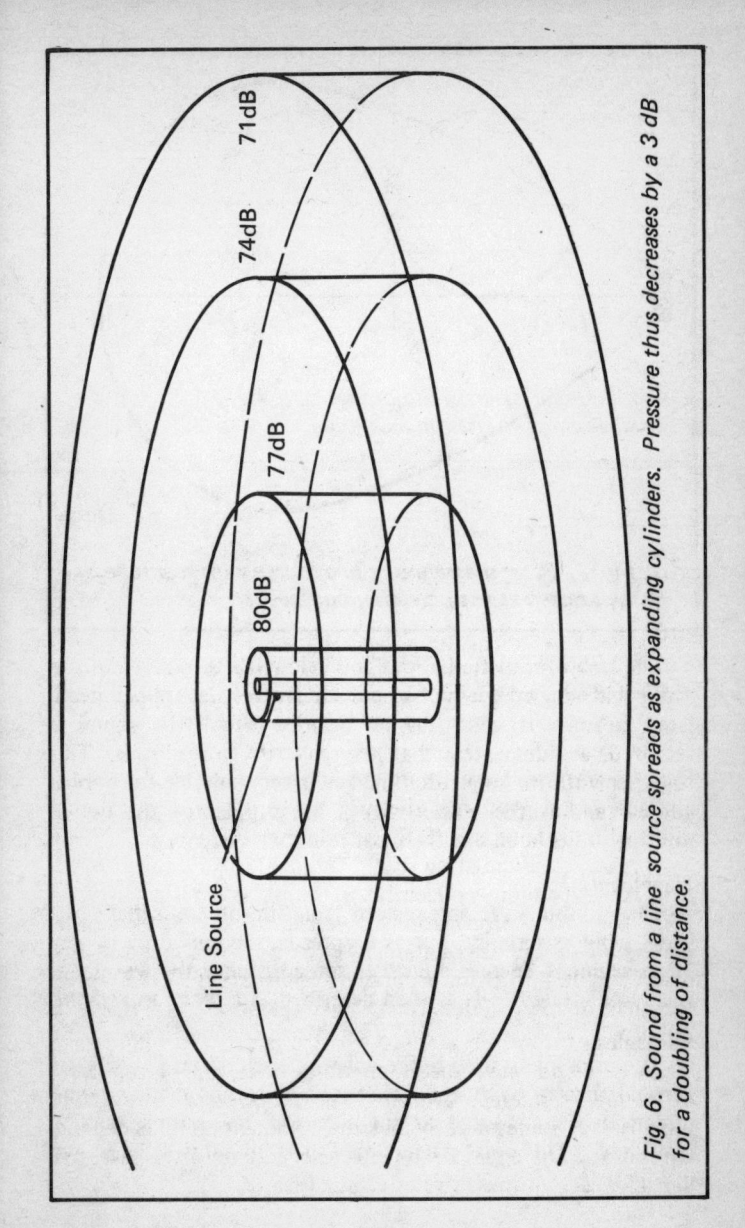

Fig. 6. Sound from a line source spreads as expanding cylinders. Pressure thus decreases by a 3 dB for a doubling of distance.

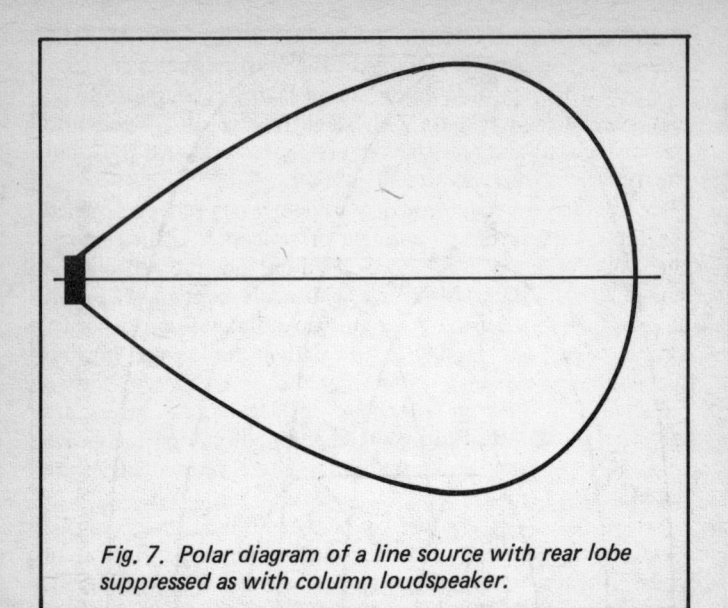

Fig. 7. Polar diagram of a line source with rear lobe suppressed as with column loudspeaker.

The lack of radiation above and below the column results in a flat wide-angled beam of sound similar to a flat-topped headlamp beam. It can thus be beamed where the sound is required, avoiding areas that may give rise to feedback. This together with its long reach, makes it very suitable for public-address and is the reason why it has supplanted the use of multiple units in all but the most primitive systems.

Wavefronts

When a sound wave spreads out from its source, initially the wave front is circular, but as it spreads, the curvature of any given segment decreases until at some distance the wavefront is almost straight. It is then described as a *plane wavefront*.

Obstacles

When a sound wave meets an obstacle it can be *reflected*, *diffracted*, *refracted*, *absorbed*, or *transmitted* through it. Usually it is some of each, but the dominant effect is dependant on the material of the obstacle and its size. We will consider each of these five effects in turn.

Reflection occurs when the surface is hard and smooth. Ceramic tile on concrete is one of the most reflective surfaces, but bare concrete, and stone are all highly reflective. Brick, and plaster on brick are only slightly less so. Wood also reflects sound, and the thicker the more reflective it is, but the thickest is less reflective than brick.

Sound waves behave similarly to light when reflected. When meeting a flat surface, the angle of reflection is the same as the angle of incidence. So a head-on meeting reflects the sound straight back, whereas a wide-angle contact reflects it at the same wide angle. A sound wave directed into a corner always comes out parallel to the path it took going in, irrespective of the angle.

When impinging in a convex surface, sound waves are scattered in all directions, but when encountering a concave one, they converge at some point. These various angles are illustrated in Figure 8.

Another effect of reflection is that a ghost image can be created which appears to be behind the reflecting surface at an equal distance to that of the source in front of it (see Fig. 9). This can cause interference and comb-filter effects.

Diffraction occurs when a sound wave encounters an edge. It flows around it, but only if the wavelength is large compared to the smallest dimension of the obstruction. If the wavelength is short the object appears large in comparison, and so casts an acoustic shadow (Fig. 10). Diffraction does not commence sharply at a particular frequency, but increases with the wavelength. At a frequency of 246/d in which d is the dimension of the shortest side in feet, the sound pressure behind the obstruction is −3 dB. At a frequency of 985/d the pressure is −10 dB.

It follows from this that the object reflects short wavelengths that are not diffracted, but not long ones which flow around it. There could thus be high-frequency reflections from structural beams and pillars.

The effect must be considered when designing reflectors or baffles. They must be large enough to be effective at the lowest frequency it is desired to reproduce.

A similar effect occurs if the sound wave encounters a hole. When the wavelength is long compared to the size of the

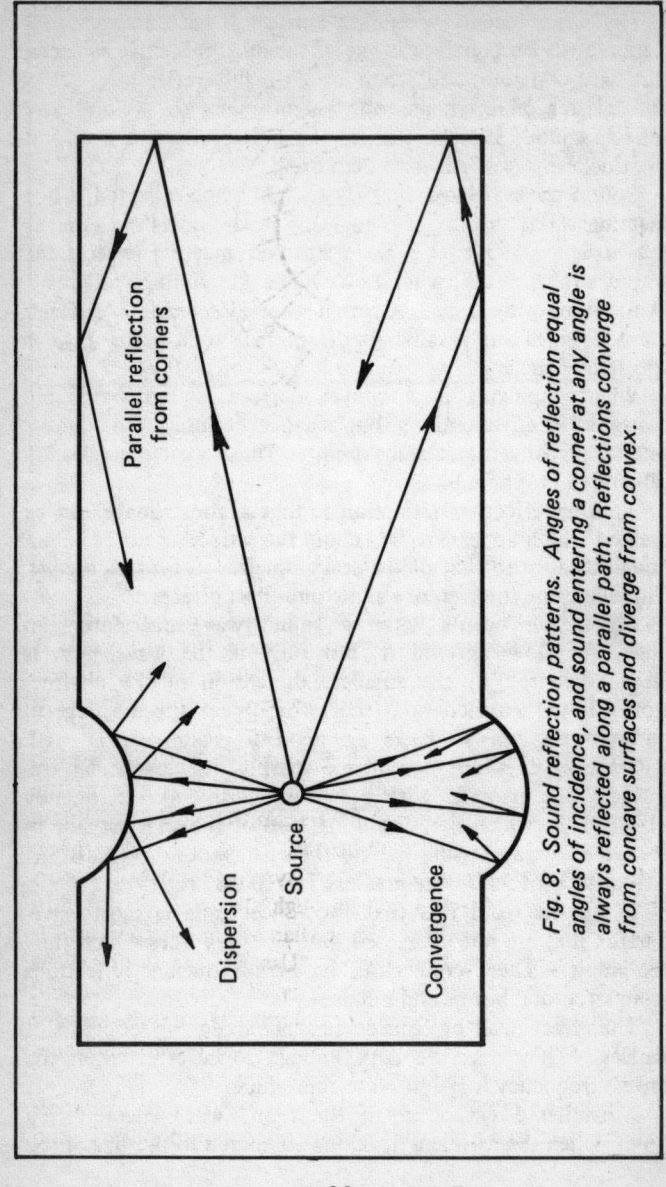

Fig. 8. Sound reflection patterns. Angles of reflection equal angles of incidence, and sound entering a corner at any angle is always reflected along a parallel path. Reflections converge from concave surfaces and diverge from convex.

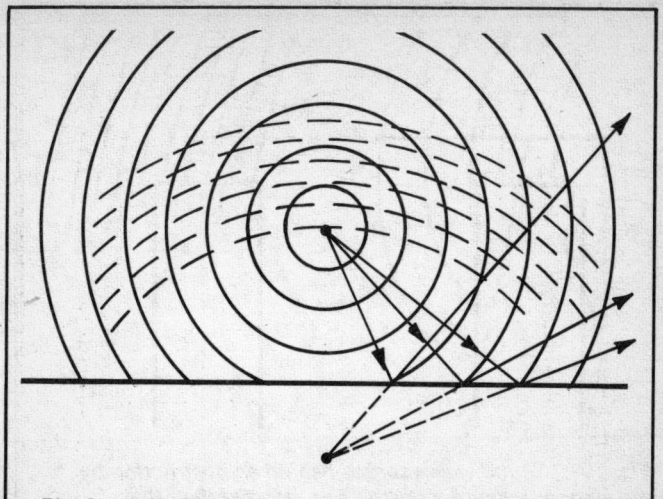

Fig. 9. Reflections from a large surface near to the source produce a ghost image behind the surface.

hole, it passes through and diffracts around it in a hemisphere. Even if the oncoming sound is a plane wave, the hole produces a circular wavefront as though the hole was a new source.

When the wavelength is short compared to the hole size it beams through, but does not diffract (Fig. 11).

Refraction takes place when a sound wave passes from a medium of one density into another. This is due to the different sound velocities; it is transmitted more slowly in the denser medium, and bends into it.

In the case of a public-address system, refraction occurs when the sound wave passes through air layers of different temperature. Cold air is denser than warm, so the wave is refracted into the colder region. Usually, the floor area is cold while the air near the ceiling is very warm, so a sound wave propagated from vertical columns is bent downward toward the audience and away from the upper walls and ceiling.

Absorption results when sound waves encounter materials that are soft and thick. Curtains, carpets, upholstery, and

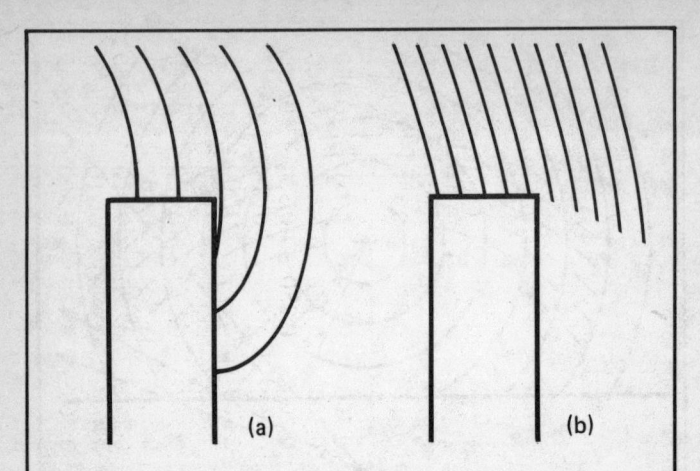

Fig. 10a. Sound waves spread behind an obstruction by diffraction when the obstruction is larger than the wavelength.

Fig. 10b. If the wavelength is shorter there is little diffraction and an acoustic shadow is cast by the object.

clothing are the most common. Acoustic panelling and tiles that have high absorption are used where sound deadening is required. The energy is dissipated in the material in the form of heat although the amount is too small to be significant. Some sound may be reflected, but some also is transmitted through the material.

The amount of absorption varies with frequency, most materials absorb mid or high frequencies more than low ones, but there are exceptions. Materials having a thin dense skin may reflect high frequencies while the softer core absorbs the low; plasterboard is an example.

In the table on page 23 reflective materials are listed in the top part and absorbents in the bottom, with their absorption coefficients at various frequencies. Maximum absorption is 1.0 which is equivalent to an open window; maximum reflection is denoted by 0, per square ft. Items marked * are for single units.

Table of Reflective and Absorbent Materials

Material	125Hz	250Hz	500Hz	1kHz	2kHz	4kHz
Brick	0.024	0.025	0.030	0.040	0.050	0.070
Concrete	0.010	0.010	0.020	0.020	0.020	0.030
Glass	0.030	0.030	0.030	0.030	0.020	0.020
Plasterboard	0.300		0.100		0.040	
Plaster on brick	0.024	0.027	0.030	0.037	0.039	0.034
Plywood $\frac{3}{8}$-inch	0.110		0.120		0.100	
Plywood $\frac{3}{16}$-inch on 2-inch batten	0.350	0.250	0.200	0.150	0.050	0.050
Wood $\frac{3}{4}$-inch solid	0.100	0.110	0.100	0.080	0.080	0.110
Acoustic panelling	0.150	0.300	0.750	0.850	0.750	0.400
Acoustic tiles $\frac{3}{4}$-inch thick	0.100	0.350	0.700	0.750	0.650	0.500
Carpet, thin	0.050	0.100	0.200	0.250	0.300	0.350
Carpet, thick with underlay	0.150		0.350		0.500	
Chair, padded upright*	1.000		2.500		0.300	
Chair, upholstered*	2.500	3.000	3.000	3.000	3.000	4.000
Curtains, light	0.050	0.120	0.150	0.270	0.370	0.500
Curtains, heavy in folds	0.200		0.500		0.800	
Fibreglass 2-inch	0.190	0.510	0.790	0.920	0.820	0.780
Fibreglass 4-inch	0.380	0.890	0.960	0.980	0.810	0.870
Person seated*	0.180	0.400	0.460	0.460	0.500	0.460

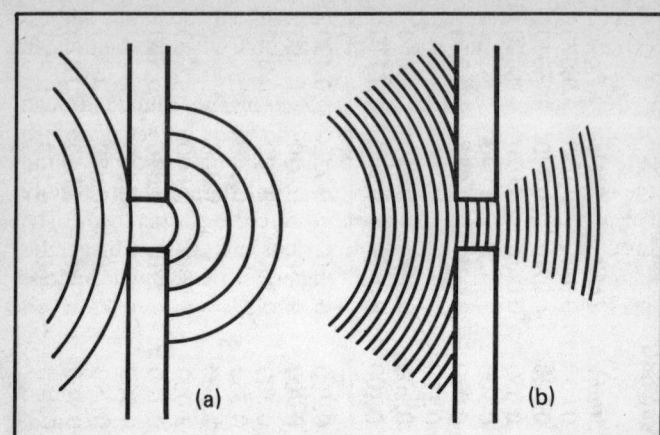

Fig. 11a. Sound waves are diffracted when passing through a hole if it is smaller than the wavelength. The hole behaves as a new source, producing spherical wavefronts even when the originating waves are plane.

Fig. 11b. At short wavelengths compared to the hole size, diffraction does not occur, resulting in a beam of sound.

Special absorbers are often used in recording studios consisting of a panel supported by its edges away from a wall. It vibrates at its resonant frequency thereby absorbing energy, however, its vibrations re-radiate part of the energy so that its absorption coefficient is always less than 0.5. Damping material placed between the panel and the wall reduce the vibrations and so increase the absorption.

Perforated panels have the effect of each hole behaving as a small resonator. Varying the hole sizes and their spacings broadens the range of frequencies absorbed, and further broadening is obtained by filling the space between panel and wall with fibreglass.

Membrane resonators are formed by placing a membrane such as roofing felt between the panel and the filling. This has the effect of lowering the resonant frequency; a double layer lowers it further.

Such devices are unlikely to be required for public-address systems in halls, but it is as well to know what can be done in case an unusual need may arise.

Transmission. Most materials transmit sound through them to a greater or lesser degree as well as reflect or absorb it. The absorbers usually transmit more airborne sound reaching them than the reflectors. But the reflectors readily transmit sound when the source is in contact with them. The study of transmission through various materials is of greater interest to sound insulation engineers than public-address operators.

Reverberation

When an enclosed space has a lot of reflective surfaces, sound bounces around for quite a while after the original has stopped, before it dies away. This is known as *reverberation*, and the time it takes for the sound pressure to die to a thousandth of its original level (-60 dB) is termed the *reverberation time.* It has a major effect on the quality of the sound.

This can be demonstrated by making a recording of speech in a bathroom where there are plenty of reflective surfaces, and following it with another in a bedroom where most of the surfaces are absorbent. Playing them back one after the other clearly demonstrates the effects of the two conditions. The reverberant recording sounds lively but not easy to follow, whereas the other sounds rather dead although the speech is clearer.

Some reverberation gives body and fullness and is especially needed for music which sounds thin without it. The optimum amount varies with the type of music and the size of the hall, but from 1.75 to 2.5 seconds is considered to be about right.

Less is needed for speech, from 0.5 to 0.75 seconds being sufficient to give it body without creating confusion.

Actually, reverberation is highly complex as it is the result of a multitude of reflections from many different surfaces at different distances. It varies with frequency, as does also the shape of the decay curves. It can alter with a change of location in the same hall.

The amount of reverberation in a public-address system also varies with the distance between the microphone and the person using it. Reverberation is picked up and re-cycled just as feedback is, so for any given volume setting it is a fixed level. The volume level of a speaker's voice though depends on his distance from the microphone, the closer, the louder. Close speaking thus gives a bigger ratio between direct sound from the speaker's voice and reflected sound from the auditorium, than distant speaking which gives a greater proportion of reflected sound.

In this chapter we have explored enough of the basic principles of acoustics to give us a good idea of how the sound behaves in a hall when a public-address system is operating. We will refer to these in subsequent chapters as we discuss how feedback can be controlled and also speech clarity improved.

Chapter 3

THE FEEDBACK PATH

There are two paths that sound from the loudspeakers can take to reach the microphone, direct and indirect. The direct one is a straight line between the two and the easiest to control; it occurs when the microphone is facing directly into the loudspeaker.

Although usually placed in front of the speaker's rostrum, the microphone could be moved to any point on the platform if interviews or demonstrations are on the programme, or if the speaker uses charts or models to illustrate his presentation. So all parts of the platform should be out of sight of a direct frontal view of the loudspeaker. The worst position is to mount loudspeakers on the back wall behind the platform (see cartoon frontispiece). Here they are facing directly into the microphone, and the path between them is short. Results would almost certainly be as illustrated!

Another poor position is to have downward facing loudspeakers mounted in the ceiling. This arrangement is a bad one for several reasons, but a direct feedback path from the line of units nearest the platform is inevitable, unless they are well back from the front, in which case the front rows of the audience are not served. In the case of the LISCA (line-source ceiling array) system, although the loudspeaker units form a row in the ceiling along the edge of the platform, they are tilted toward the audience. Having a dipole propagation pattern, the cosine of the 90° angle subtended from the units to the platform gives zero output.

A pitfall which could trap the unwary is to place loudspeaker(s) forward from the microphone, facing the audience, but in front of or just to one side of it. Such a set-up is likely with a small portable system where a single loudspeaker is placed in a central position in front of the microphone stand. It may thus appear that all the sound is being directed away from the microphone and into the audience.

The point being overlooked here is that unless it is in an airtight cabinet, the loudspeaker is a dipole and is radiating

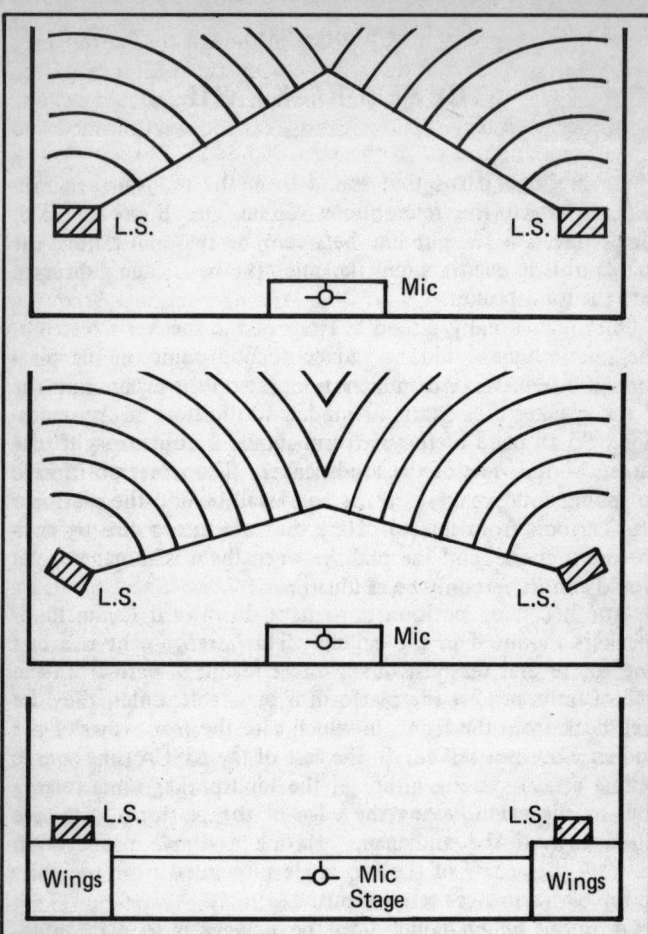

Fig. 12a. Column loudspeakers placed forward from the microphone to avoid direct feedback. A large section at the middle of the hall is not covered.

Fig. 12b. Turning the loudspeakers slightly inward covers the central area. If the sides are kept toward the microphone there will be no direct feedback.

Fig. 12c. Side facades to a stage make ideal mounting positions for column loudspeakers.

from the rear as well as the front. Although the output may be less from the rear due to the acoustic resistance of the cabinet back, there is still output from it. So the microphone is located within the loudspeaker's rear propagation lobe and is also close to it.

Loudspeakers should be positioned to the side, slightly forward and angled inward to give coverage to the centre of the audience. For columns, a location on the side walls of the hall is usually the most convenient. The inward angle should not be so great though as to bring the microphone within the field of propagation (see Fig. 12).

With a wide auditorium, a pair of columns on the platform rear wall is permissible if they are placed well away from the platform itself. Although being behind the line of the microphone, the angle from the front of the loudspeakers to the microphone is so wide as to be almost in their region of zero output (Fig. 7).

A stage with a facade affords an excellent mounting position as this gives good audience coverage at the centre, yet has no direct line-of-sight path to the microphone (Fig. 12c).

Indirect Path

The direct path as we have seen, can be easily controlled by judicious placement of the loudspeakers. A glance is sufficient to see whether an existing system has any direct paths or not, and if so how they can be eliminated. Feedback from direct paths should therefore never happen, at least not with knowledgeable operators!

The indirect path is another matter. It cannot be completely eliminated in any system that has loudspeakers and microphones operating in the same air mass. The goal must therefore be to reduce the coupling to as low a level as possible.

The indirect path arises from multiple sound reflections around the auditorium. Mostly these are from walls, especially the back wall, but they also are produced from vacant unpadded chair backs, pillars, doors and any other reflective surface. The floor can also produce strong reflections especially from downward facing ceiling loudspeakers, even if it is carpeted.

As the table of absorbent coefficients (page 23) shows, the thin carpeting likely to be used for public halls has an absorption coefficient of around 0.25 at mid-frequencies, which means it absorbs only 25% of the sound reaching it. Most of the 75% remaining is transmitted through it to be reflected from the floor beneath. On the return transmission a further 25% of the 75% is absorbed leaving some 56% of the original sound to be reflected back into the auditorium.

All this mish-mash of reflected sound radiates back to the platform and the microphone. We shall discuss microphone details in the next chapter, but for the time being we shall just assume that a directional microphone is in use. It rejects sound coming from the rear, and to a lesser extent the sides, favouring that coming from the front.

The Platform Wall

It would thus seem that as sound from the auditorium arriving at the rear of the microphone is rejected, indirect feedback could be eliminated. The big snag is the wall behind the platform. All auditorium sound is collected by it and reflected right into the front of the microphone. Being only a few feet away, the reflection is strong and the feedback large.

The solution though is not difficult. It is to cover the wall with sound absorbent material. Looking back at the absorbent chart we find that 4-inch fibreglass has the largest absorbent coefficient, but it would hardly serve as a practical wall covering! Fortunately, there are other more practical materials. Acoustic tiles or panelling are possibilities as they have high absorbent coefficients.

Curtains

A more common solution and an excellent one, is heavy curtains. These are visually attractive as well as having high absorption coefficients. For maximum effectiveness they should hang in deep folds, and a lining also helps. The absorption coefficient is from 0.5 to 0.8 over the mid frequencies, which means that a sound wave reflected from the rear wall has to pass through the curtain twice and so is attenuated from 0.25 to 0.16 of its former pressure. Further absorption could be obtained if desired by lining the wall over the central area behind the microphone, with acoustic or cork tiles.

The curtains should be from ceiling to floor and extend across the complete wall or at least over the whole of the platform area. Random sound arriving from the auditorium comes from all angles. Some is reflected from a side wall, to be again reflected from the back wall into the microphone at a point well to its side (Fig. 13). This shows why the curtains should extend completely across the wall and not just that part immediately in front of the microphone. The whole surface can reflect sound into it depending on the angles of arrival.

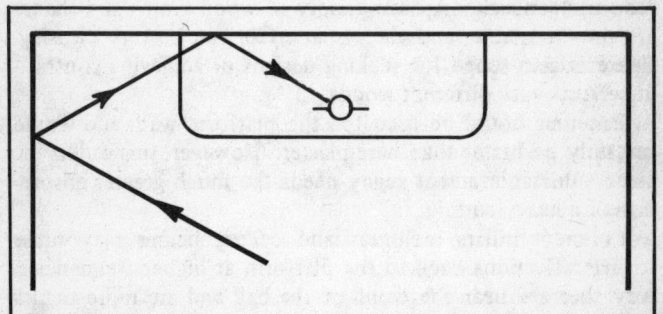

Fig. 13. Reflections can enter a microphone from the side of the back wall, so absorbent treatment should be extended over the whole wall.

If further absorbent treatment is desired on the wall behind the curtain, it can be confined to the central area. The reason is that reflections from the sides have to pass sideways through the curtain and its many folds, and do so twice. They are thus virtually completely suppressed without further need of absorbent.

The beneficial effect of curtaining the platform wall over its whole length cannot be emphasized too strongly. Many installations are known where feedback was hopeless and the purchase of expensive new equipment was planned in the hope of curing it. The advice to curtain a bare platform wall was met with some scepticism which turned to astonishment when it was carried out and feedback problems all but disappeared. Suitable microphones are also necessary as we shall see later.

Wood Panelling

Most of the sound arriving at the platform has been reflected many times from the side and rear walls which are usually plaster on brick or plaster on cement blocks. A useful reduction of reflected sound from these can be made by decorating the walls with thin wood panelling suspended on wooden laths. These panels absorb lower frequencies resulting in a clear acoustic which improves speech intelligibility, and reduces feedback. A wide variety of wood grains and shades are now available, and the visual effect can be very pleasing. There is also scope for making designs or achieving contrasting effects with different woods.

Panelling could be used for the platform wall, and would certainly be better than bare plaster. However, this wall is the most vulnerable and it really needs the much greater absorption of a heavy curtain.

Concrete pillars, columns and ceiling beams may cause strong reflections back to the platform at higher frequencies. Any that are near the front of the hall and are more than a few inches wide could be covered on the side facing the platform with a convenient absorbent.

Loudspeaker Tilting

We have already discussed the positioning and horizontal angling of loudspeakers in order to avoid direct-path feedback. In the case of vertical columns, they can be mounted somewhat higher than audience-head height and tilted forward to beam into the audience (Fig. 14). This makes full use of the flat-topped-and-bottomed beam effect of these loudspeakers.

Even when used with the bottom of the column at audience shoulder height and in the upright position, the flat beam top avoids reflections from the upper walls and ceiling. But the forward tilt prevents almost all reflection from the back wall.

Occasionally, installations are seen in which column loudspeakers are mounted high and upright. They thus beam the

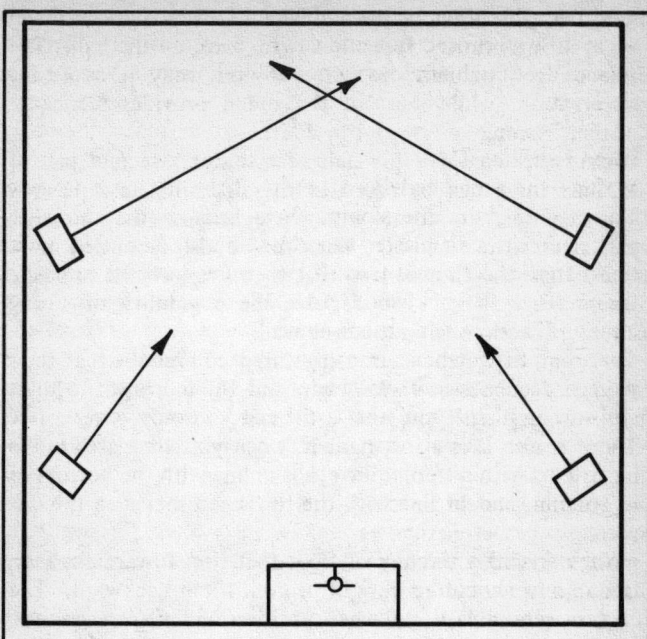

Fig. 14a. Where two pairs of column loudspeakers are used, the rear pair should be directed toward the rear corners to minimise reflection.

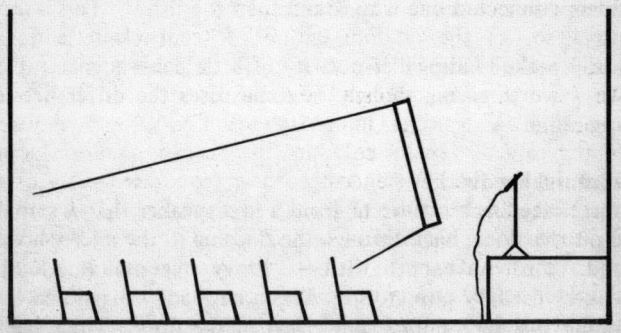

Fig. 14b. Tilting a column forward reduces reflections from the back wall of the hall. The height and tilt must be so arranged to ensure front and back rows are in the sound beam.

sound over the heads of the audience to hit the back wall and give a strong primary reflection right back up the hall. The audience get virtually no direct sound, only a confusing reverberation, while most of the sound provides feedback! Another example of how not to do it!

When the length of the hall necessitates a second pair of columns, these can be tilted as the first, in fact it is even more beneficial to do so with these because they are that much nearer the rear wall. They should also be angled more inward than the first pair so that they fire into the opposite corners (Fig. 14b). This reduces the possibility of strong primary reflections from the back wall.

A point to watch when using tilted columns is that their coverage decreases as their height and tilt increases. Mount them too high with too great a tilt and you only cover a few rows of seats. It is about right if, when you are seated in the first row to be covered, your eye is in line with the bottom of the column, and in line with the top when seated in the last row.

When serving a balcony or floor that rises toward the rear, the columns should be upright or even tilted backward. The eye test should indicate when position and tilt are correct.

Loudspeaker Phasing

It is sometimes found that feedback is less with the loudspeaker feeders connected one way round than the other. This is not always so, as the random nature of feedback reflections usually make loudspeaker polarity of little consequence. It is always worth trying though, in some cases the difference is appreciable.

Structural Feedback

Indirect feedback can occur from a loudspeaker that is standing on the floor, back through the flooring to the microphone stand. This can happen with the heavy stage-standing loudspeakers used by pop groups. It can be readily diagnosed by holding the microphone stand clear of the floor. Thick pads under the loudspeakers should cure it, and/or a pad under the microphone stand.

Chapter 4

MICROPHONES AND FEEDBACK

The choice of microphone has a considerable effect on feedback, in fact apart from the platform wall curtain it is the greatest single factor affecting it. Microphones are classified according to the type of transducer and also their directivity or polar response. For public-address purposes, there are three types of transducers:

Moving-coil

The moving-coil type of microphone has a construction similar to that of a loudspeaker. A shallow plastic cone has a small coil wound on a former at its apex which lies within the two concentric poles of a magnet. Sound pressure waves cause the cone to vibrate and this induces corresponding voltages in the coil.

The coils have an impedance of 30Ω which is rather low to directly drive the input of most mixers. A built-in transformer raises the impedance to 200Ω, 600Ω or 50kΩ, hence also the output voltages. The 50kΩ impedance gives a high output but suffers from loss of treble over long cables due to cable capacitance. It is only suitable for cable lengths of up to 6 feet (2 m).

The transducer is very robust and will stand a lot of hard knocks, which makes it attractive for many portable systems. Its main snag is a resonance peak in its frequency response at around 2 kHz, which is due to the combined mass of the cone and coil.

The peak gives a 'bright' tone which is favoured by many users. It emphasizes random background noise which is usually centred around this frequency, hence the term *presence effect* used by some makers to describe it. For public-address use though, the peak is a definite disadvantage as it encourages feedback, as we shall see later.

Ribbon

Ribbon microphones have a narrow corrugated aluminium ribbon supported between the poles of a powerful magnet.

It is not pressure actuated because both front and back of the ribbon are exposed to the air, so the pressure is the same at both sides. Instead it is moved by the velocity of air particles as they rush back and forth past the ribbon. That is why it is often described as a *velocity microphone*. Signal voltages are generated by the ribbon moving in the magnetic field.

Impedance is very low, a fraction of an ohm, so an inbuilt transformer is always used to give an output impedance of $200\Omega - 600\Omega$. The mass of the ribbon is much lower than that of the moving coil, so it responds readily to high frequencies and fast transients. This also produces a resonance that it is out of, or toward the upper limit of the normal frequency range. The resulting frequency response is very smooth with no peaks, which inhibits feedback when used for public-address work.

Ribbon microphones are less robust than the moving-coil instrument and must be treated with respect, although they stand up well to normal usage. They tend to be expensive and few makers produce them. One such is Beyer and their M260 ribbon has been a first choice for many public-address buffs for a number of years.

Electret

The electret is the poor relation of the professional capacitor microphone. In the capacitor unit a thin plastic diaphragm coated with aluminium or gold is stretched over a shallow cavity having a flat metal backplate. It thus forms a capacitor. Sound pressure waves move the diaphragm thus varying the spacing between it and the backplate, and thereby also the capacitance. A high polarizing voltage is applied to attract the diaphragm to the backplate and so keep it taut. As the capacitance changes with sound pressure, charging and discharging currents flow.

These currents produce varying voltage drops over a high-value resistor, that correspond to the diaphragm excursions, hence the sound wave pressures. The impedance of the device is very high and if applied to a microphone cable all treble would be lost over just a few inches. So the microphone must have a built-in amplifier to serve as an impedance converter. The polarizing voltage, usually 50V, must be supplied from the mixer and conveyed to the microphone along the cable.

The diaphragm is very light and free from resonances over its operating range so giving a virtually flat frequency response, and an excellent response to high frequencies. It is the chief instrument used in recording and broadcast studios, but its high cost and the need for the polarizing voltage precludes its use for all but the most exotic public-address systems.

The electret works on exactly the same principle, but an electrostatic charge which is equivalent to around a 100V polarizing voltage, is implanted into the diaphragm during manufacture. The need for an external voltage is thus avoided. This charge leaks away in time, but its half-life is said to be up to 100 years. It can be much sooner though if the instrument is subject to excessive damp.

A built-in amplifier is required, but this usually takes the form of a single transistor powered by a 1½V battery. All electret microphones thus have an internal torch cell and a switch to turn it on and off.

The diaphragm has to be thicker than that of the capacitor microphone in order to hold the charge, so its mass is greater and its resonant frequency lower. It thus encroaches into the operating frequency range, however, with some models it is still quite high at around 8 kHz. This is much higher than the average moving-coil unit, and it can be tamed with a little top-cut from the tone controls.

Low cost compared to the ribbon is a big plus, and if the model is well chosen good results with low feedback is possible. The main problem with these is that the switch and battery contacts can become noisy.

Polar Response

The response to sounds coming from different directions is the second way that microphones are classified. The three most commonly used are:

Omni-directional. The back of the diaphragm is sealed and not open to free air. These microphones are thus sensitive to sound pressures at the surface of the diaphragm, irrespective of the direction of the source. The exception is for sound waves coming from behind that have wavelengths shorter than the diaphragm radius. These do not diffract around the diaphragm and so exert no pressure on it.

The response to sounds coming from all directions is therefore the same for low and mid-range frequencies, but it becomes increasingly directional as the frequency ascends.

Cardioid. These have an air duct from the back of the diaphragm to the open air, which contains an acoustic resistance. Sound pressure thus affects both sides of the diaphragm, but when facing the sound source, pressure on the front of the diaphragm is reinforced by air particle velocity. A pressure gradient thus exists between the front and back of the diaphragm which moves in response.

Although exposed to free air, the back surface of the diaphragm is masked by the housing and the acoustic resistance. This shields it from direct particle velocity from sound waves arriving from the rear. Equal pressure is thereby exerted on both sides of the diaphragm, and no movement results.

So the microphone responds to sounds from the front but gives reducing output as the off-axis angle increases, to become zero at the back. At 90°, the output is around 6 dB less than the on-axis value.

The polar response is thus shaped like a heart, hence the name cardioid. The terms *pressure gradient* and *velocity* are also applied.

Super/hyper cardioid. These terms are often used interchangeably although they are not the same. Reducing the acoustic resistance in the rear air path of a cardioid, increases the pressure at the back of the diaphragm from sounds arriving from the side. The pressure gradient is thus decreased and the output reduced. So the response to side sounds is less than the cardioid thereby making a narrower, more directional frontal polar response. This is the super-cardioid.

If the resistance is decreased further, the side response is reduced still more to around −10 dB, but some particle velocity from rear-arriving sound now gains access to the back of the diaphragm. As a result, a small lobe of about −12 dB appears at the rear of the response plot and the device becomes a hypercardioid.

Directivity

In spite of the small pickup at the rear where the cardioid has none, the reduced side sensitivity at all sides, gives an overall greater rejection of non-frontal sounds than the cardioid.

If an omni, cardioid and hypercardioid microphone are placed facing a sound source in a reverberant sound field, the cardioid will pick up 0.58 of the total field received by the omni, and the hypercardioid only 0.5 of it. Put another way, for a given feedback level, the cardioid can be placed 1.73 times the distance from the source as the omni, while the hypercardioid can be placed twice as far.

As the reflections which cause feedback come from all directions it is the overall rejection which is important; clearly the hypercardioid rejects the most and so is best for reducing feedback. If the cardioid is used sideways toward the auditorium such as for interviews, its low side rejection of only 6 dB can give rise to feedback, or poor intelligibility due to a high degree of reverberation. The omni-directional microphone is very poor for feedback, and of little use for public-address.

If data may not be available for a particular model, although the style of microphone housings differ considerably, it is usually possible to distinguish between an omni and a cardioid. The omni has no vents in the side, whereas the others have. Distinguishing a cardioid from a hypercardioid is less certain. The vents in the later are often larger than the cardioid but this can vary with different models.

Ball-ended microphones are usually cardioids or hypercardioids, the rear air access being through the base of the ball.

While the choice of a hypercardioid is a step in the right direction for reducing feedback, it is only half the story. There is another important microphone characteristic which must be considered. We will deal with this in the next chapter.

Chapter 5

PEAKS AND NOTCHES

Every public-address system has its own particular *feedback level*. This is the maximum amount of gain that can be used before feedback commences. The objective is to make it as high as possible, and each of the factors that have so far been discussed will either raise it or lower it according to what action has been taken.

Using hypercardioid microphones raises the level compared to what it would be with cardioids or omnis; using properly angled column loudspeakers or the LISCA system gives a higher feedback level than other loudspeaker arrangements. A large increase in level results from curtaining the rear platform wall, and so on.

Thus it can be seen that the solution is not one single factor but is a combination of many, every one contributes to the overall level and any item neglected or inadequately executed pulls the level down.

Having achieved as high a level as we can, what effect can be expected? In Figure 15 the feedback level of a system is plotted on a gain/frequency chart. If the amplifier gain is turned up to the point shown in (a), operation is just below feedback, and ringing is very likely. The slightest change in operation, such as someone on the platform turning a directional hand microphone toward the auditorium, will make the system go over the top.

To obtain stability and stop ringing or *incipient feedback* as it is technically termed, the gain must be reduced to the point shown in (b). It should be noted that it is always better to sacrifice some volume and opt for lower gain in order to avoid ringing which degrades intelligibility and is uncomfortable to listen to.

The curve shown in (b) then is the normal operating point for a system that has a flat frequency response throughout its range. Unfortunately this is almost never the case. Even good quality microphones of public-address standard have peaks in their response and this is especially true of moving-coil instruments.

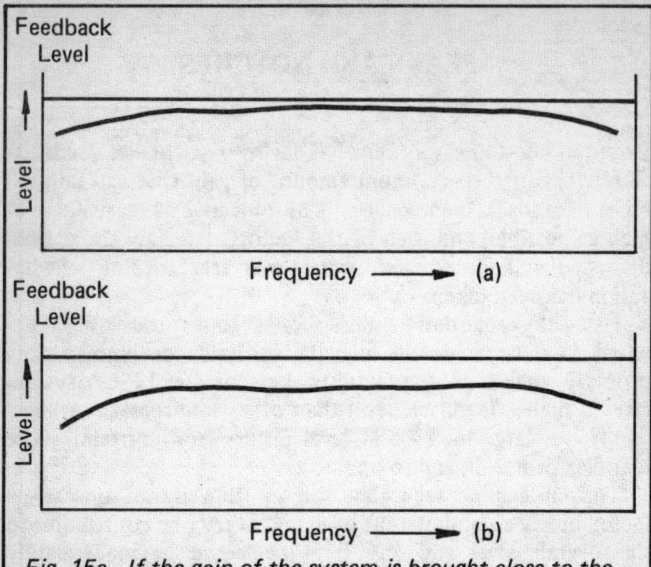

Fig. 15a. If the gain of the system is brought close to the feedback level, ringing occurs and feedback may take place without warning.

Fig. 15b. For clarity and safety, the gain must be well below the feedback level.

Loudspeaker cones also have fundamental resonances that cause peaks in their response, and both these and that of the microphone, have harmonics, that is resonances at twice, three times, four times, etc., the frequency of the fundamental.

Added to these are troughs and peaks which are the result of comb filter effects due to reflections or multiple loudspeaker sources in the auditorium.

The result is a frequency response that is far from the nice flat curves depicted in Figure 15. It is more like those shown in Figure 16. Notice with the curve shown in (a) that the largest peak has just exceeded the feedback level. The system will therefore go into violent feedback. Yet note also where the average volume level lies — well below the feedback level. To avoid feedback, the gain must be dropped to the point shown in (b), and the average gain level is thus shifted even further down.

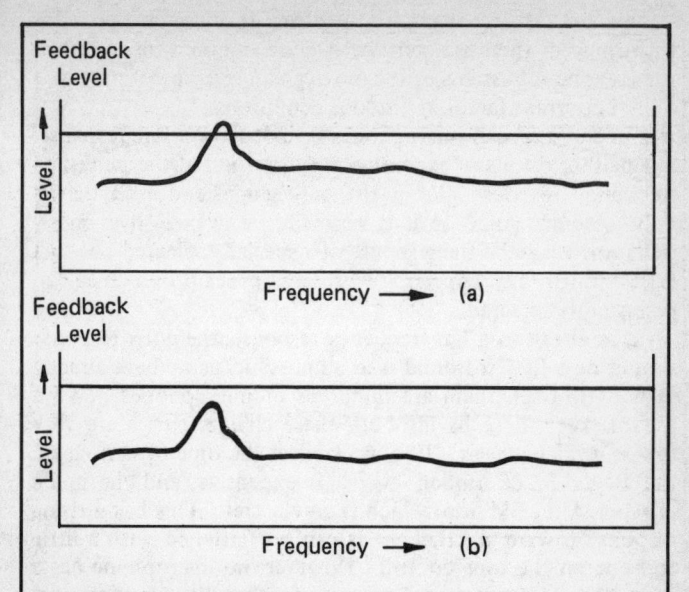

Fig. 16a. All systems have peaks. If only the tip exceeds feedback level, feedback will occur, even though the overall level is well below it.

Fig. 16b. To keep the peak below feedback level, the overall level must be lower still. Usable gain thus depends on the height of the largest system peak.

So it can be seen that peaks in the response reduce the amount of gain that can be used by an amount equal to their amplitude. In addition to achieving a high feedback level, killing feedback requires reducing system peaks as far as possible.

Microphone Response

Usually, the largest peak is due to the microphone, this being the factor mentioned in the last chapter that should be investigated before choosing any particular model. Moving-coil instruments nearly all have a resonance peak due to the combined mass of the coil and diaphragm. They are therefore, not a good choice for indoor public-address systems. Outdoor set-ups are a different matter, feedback is not such a problem with these as there is no enclosed space and no walls to reflect sound. The robustness of the moving-coil instrument may be a more important factor in outdoor conditions.

Generally, cheap microphones do not have a flat response, but neither do many expensive ones. Perusal of the published frequency response plot is the only guide, and even that is only a rough guide as it is normally an average over many units, or it may be the response of a specially selected one. At least though, any appearing with large peaks on its chart can be instantly rejected.

In addition to a flat frequency response, the polar response should be a hypercardioid if at all possible, as we have already seen. Although there are hundreds of microphones now on the market, those having both these characteristics are very few and far between. Two available at the time of writing are the Beyer M260 ribbon, which is expensive, and the much cheaper Altai EM 506, which is an electret. This has a rising response toward 8 kHz, but it can be flattened with a little top cut on the tone control. However, no microphone has a completely flat frequency response other than professional studio capacitor units.

There are though other peaks due to loudspeakers and acoustics, as well as the minor ones appearing with even good microphones. If these could be eliminated and an overall flat response achieved, gain could be brought up to a much higher level without any part of the response curve encroaching over the feedback level.

Notches

One way of getting rid of a peak is to superimpose on it its exact inverse which is a notch of the same frequency and amplitude. This is shown in Figure 17(a) and the resultant obtained by adding the two is shown at (b) which is a level response. If such notches could be arranged for every peak, the result would be the desired flat overall frequency response.

The notch must be of exactly the same frequency or very close to it. If it is displaced by more than half the width of the peak, it has no effect on the amplitude of the peak at all.

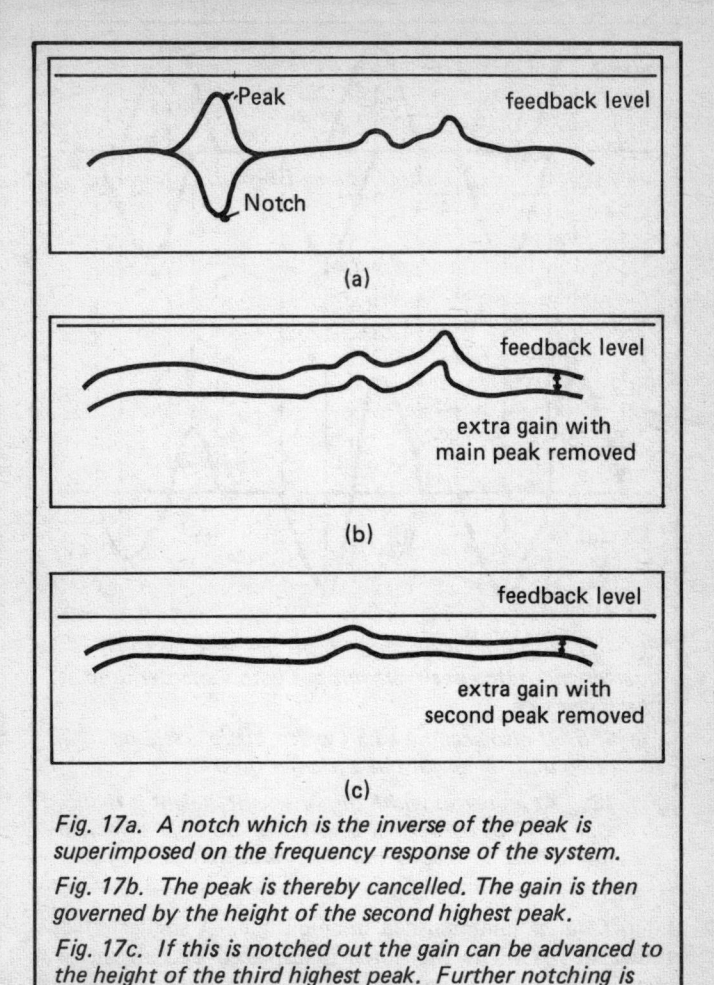

Fig. 17a. A notch which is the inverse of the peak is superimposed on the frequency response of the system.

Fig. 17b. The peak is thereby cancelled. The gain is then governed by the height of the second highest peak.

Fig. 17c. If this is notched out the gain can be advanced to the height of the third highest peak. Further notching is possible but with diminishing benefit.

The effects of displaced notches are shown in Figure 18. At (a) the notch is displaced by three-quarters of the width of the peak. The resultant shows that the peak has a sharper

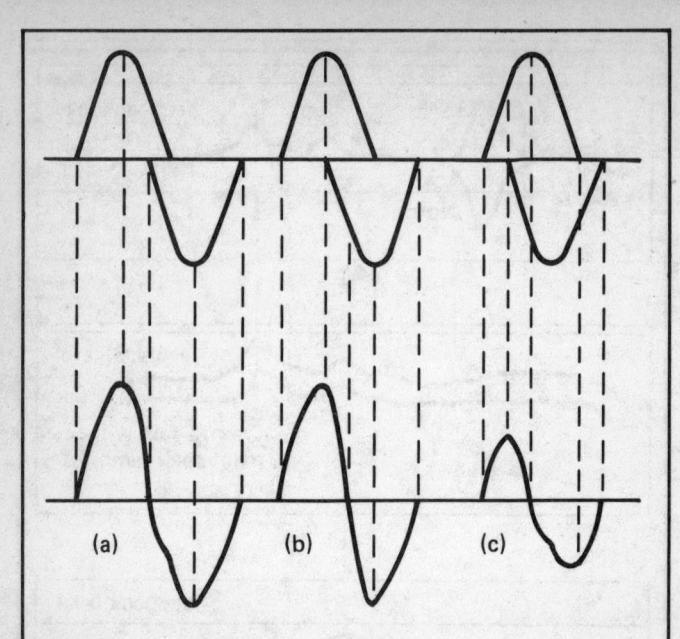

Fig. 18a. If a notch is displaced from the peak by three-quarter width, the peak remains but with a sharper drop at one lower side.

Fig. 18b. If displaced by a half width, there is still no reduction of peak height but a sharper drop.

Fig. 18c. At a quarter width displacement, height is reduced to about a half of the former amplitude. So to be effective the notch must be exactly the same frequency as the peak.

fall-off but is undiminished in amplitude. A similar effect is shown at (b) where the notch is displaced by half the peak width; the fall-off is sharper, but the peak amplitude remains the same. At (c) the notch is displaced by a quarter, and here, the peak is reduced by some 40% but is still not eliminated.

Another feature of the peak which should be considered is its width. When a physical object resonates it is not just one frequency that is emphasized, adjacent ones also are affected although to a lesser degree. The fall-off on either side of

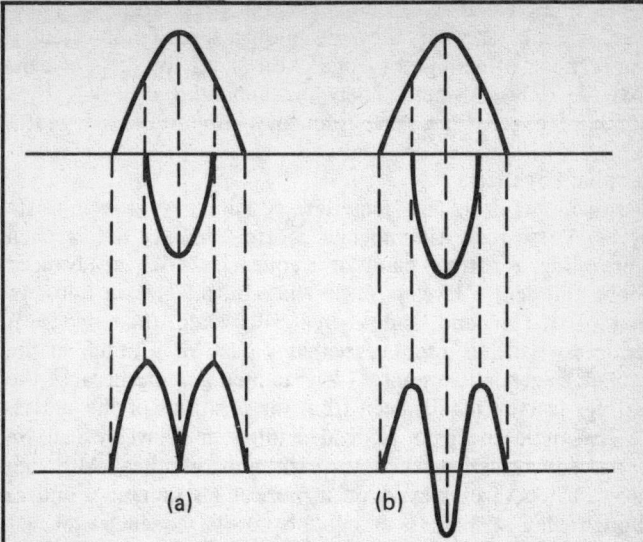

Fig. 19a. A notch of insufficient width produces two smaller peaks.

Fig. 19b. Increasing the depth of the notch only generates a well between the twin peaks. So, the notch must be as wide as well as of the same height and frequency of the peak.

resonance is usually at a rate of 6 dB per octave. If two resonances coincide, the fall-off is at 12 dB per octave, but this is uncommon.

If a notch of exactly the same frequency but with a sharper fall-off hence of a narrower width than the peak is applied, two smaller peaks are created, one on each side of the original (Fig. 19(a)). They are not affected by increasing the amplitude of the notch, this merely deepens the well between them (Fig. 19(b)). If the notch is not exactly the same frequency, the peaks will be of unequal size.

Another possibility is where there are two notches, one either side of the peak. If they are spaced so as to just overlap the peak their only effect is to narrow it. But when they are close, they merge to form a double-dip notch, and this can reduce the peak amplitude. If the notch depth is increased it can eliminate the peak entirely. However, a large area of the surrounding spectrum is thereby engulfed so affecting the tone. From all this it is evident that the only satisfactory way of eliminating a peak is by a notch of exactly the same frequency, amplitude and width.

Graphic Equalizers

Graphic equalizers are sometimes used to try to eliminate peaks. These have a number of controls, usually sliders, each controlling a narrow band of frequencies. When advanced above the centre level position, the control gives a boost to that particular band, and when it is lowered, the response is reduced. It thus produces either a peak or a notch in the overall frequency response. It is termed *graphic* because the settings can be readily seen from the positions of the sliders.

The audio spectrum is divided into ten octaves which are so named because each contains eight musical notes. Although successive octaves played on a musical instrument sound as though they encompass an equal band of frequencies, in fact they do not, this is the way they sound to our ears.

Each octave is twice the frequency of the one below it, so starting from the bottom, and with figures rounded to the nearest whole number the ten octaves are: 16 − 31 Hz; 31 − 62 Hz; 62 − 125 Hz; 125 − 250 Hz; 250 − 500 Hz; 500 − 1,000 Hz; 1 kHz − 2 kHz; 2 − 4 kHz; 4 − 8 kHz; 8 − 16 kHz.

It can thus be seen that any octave is equal in frequency range to all the octaves below it put together. Actually it is greater, because it is equal to all those plus the sub-sonic frequencies below 16 Hz.

The simplest equalizer has five bands, which means that there is only one band to two octaves. Such an instrument can do little more than enable a subjective adjustment to be made to a music system, such as one installed in a car. The chance of one of the bands coinciding exactly with a resonance peak is remote, so it is virtually useless for public-address.

A more common domestic equalizer is the ten-band model. This provides one control for each octave. For stereo this has to be doubled to twenty bands, but only mono is required for public-address. Again the resolution is insufficient. The chance that a feedback peak would exactly coincide with one of the equalizer control frequencies is only twice as great as the five-band model. The bands are too widely spaced to produce an effective double-dip elimination of a peak by adjacent bands, and any attempt to do so would take out a large chunk of the spectrum.

The equalizer used by professionals is the third-octave type, having thirty controls per channel. There is much better chance of a band coinciding with a peak, but even with this the chances are less than even of getting it exact. Should it happen, the notch may then be narrower than the peak, depending on the model used. However, there is a fairly good chance of taming the peak with two adjacent bands.

Setting up an Equalizer

To start, all controls should be at the level position. The volume is turned up until feedback occurs. Then the controls which affect the peak must be discovered. This is a matter of trial and error, which with thirty to choose from, can be rather tedious and time-consuming. However, the choice can be narrowed with a little judgement, which tends to improve with experience.

If the feedback note is a hoot, try the controls from 250 – 500 Hz. If it is a singing tone, try around 1 kHz, but if it is a whistle, go for 2 kHz and above. It is unlikely to be in the top octave 8 – 16 kHz, or the bottom two, 16 – 62 Hz.

Lower the controls in the suspected region one at a time, restoring each afterward until the feedback level changes. If more than one affects it, find the one that affects it most, as this will be the nearest channel to the peak. Turn the slider down until feedback stops and then turn up the system gain control. If feedback starts again at the same frequency take the slider further down or try an adjacent one.

Adjust the settings and that of the gain control until the feedback changes pitch. This means that the primary peak has been reduced and the next largest has taken over. Repeat the operation for this one.

It may then be found that the first peak returns. This is because it wasn't levelled but just reduced to a lower level than the second. When that one is lowered, the first peak takes over again as the largest. So further juggling and adjusting is required of both, during which a third tone may put in an appearance.

The setting up obviously requires patience, and if done in an empty hall, will likely need re-adjustment when the acoustics are changed by the arrival of the audience or when the temperature changes. Added to these drawbacks, thirty-band equalizers are not inexpensive! But there is a better way.

Variable-notch Filters

A variable-notch filter is a device that produces a notch but no boost, which for this purpose is not required. The major advantage over an equalizer is that the notch is continuously variable and so can be tuned to exactly the same frequency as the peak. Two notches are generally sufficient, each with a tuning control, but in theory any number could be cascaded. The device is smaller, less formidable, much easier to set up, is cheaper, and because it can mirror the peak exactly, is more effective than an equalizer.

Full details as to the construction of such a filter are given later and also how to use it. The described unit is a twin-notch device which enables the two largest feedback peaks to be levelled, and it has controls which enable the amplitude of the notch to match that of the peak. It has a 6 dB per octave fall-off also matching that of the resonance peak.

Apart from reducing feedback the notch filter has another useful feature. Reproduced reverberation through the system robs speech of its clarity. This tends to be greater at frequencies around the resonance peaks. This is especially so when the gain is up near the feedback level as it sometimes has to be to pick up inarticulate speakers. Raised too far, it becomes evident with the familiar decaying ringing tones.

As the notch levels out the peak, it also reduces the reverberation coming through the system. In fact, if the notch is tuned through the peak when a programme is in progress, the improvement in speech clarity becomes quite noticeable.

Another advantage is that feedback is initiated less readily when the feedback level is approached by a flat response than by a sharp peak. It behaves like a well-damped oscillatory electronic circuit. If there is no peak, when feedback level is exceeded the circuit doesn't know at what frequency to oscillate. It seeks any small remaining peak and starts to oscillate slowly and sluggishly.

In contrast a sharp peak will start things oscillating smartly, and the operator must be ever vigilant. So it is much less nerve-racking to operate with a flat response than one with peaks!

The amount of extra gain available by using notch filters depends on the peaks in the system. Greatest benefit is obtained when peaks are large, as their elimination brings a bigger increase in usable gain. Conversely, when the peaks are small there is less increase. However, all systems have peaks, so some improvement is certain, and the extra clarity and slow feedback characteristic makes the unit well worthwhile.

Before we describe the unit though, there is another useful anti-feedback device that we will discuss in the next chapter.

Chapter 6

FREQUENCY SHIFTERS

Frequency shifting is an effective way of reducing feedback, though not without its disadvantages. It works by raising all frequencies that pass through it by about 5 Hz. For speech this has no audible effect as the percentage change in pitch is too small to be noticed. However, the feedback signal does not pass through the system once, but thousands of times, rapidly. Each time round its frequency is raised by 5 Hz, so it does not reinforce itself and is quickly shifted away from the resonant peaks, being soon pushed to above the audible range.

The effect when the gain is taken up to the feedback level is that of a succession of bleeps, each ascending in pitch, like some car alarms, rather than the continuous howl normally obtained.

How They Work

There is more than one way of achieving frequency shift, although all have certain things in common. One method is as follows:

The input signal is split into two paths and by the choice of the values of coupling components the two signals are in quadrature at all frequencies (90° out of phase). A quadrature sine wave oscillator running at a frequency of 5 Hz has two outputs that are also 90° out of phase.

Each audio signal is multiplied in a quadrature multiplier, by a different 5 Hz output. This produces sum and difference signals in each path consisting of the audio plus 5 Hz, and audio minus 5 Hz.

With the minus signals, we have a −90° phase difference between the two audio signals to start with, and a +90° difference between the two oscillator outputs. When subtracted these produce a total shift of −180°, so that the minus signals in the two paths are out of phase.

With the sum signals there is a +90° signal difference between the audio signals and a −90° difference between the oscillator outputs. These, when added, give a zero difference so that the two plus signals are in phase.

The two paths then are combined so that the out-of-phase difference signals cancel each other, whereas the in-phase sum signals reinforce. The output thus consists only of the sum signal of the original audio plus 5 Hz.

Careful adjustment of preset controls are required to ensure the circuits are balanced and the two signals are of equal amplitude; also the oscillator must be accurately adjusted.

Advantages

The device enables up to 6 dB extra gain to be obtained before feedback which is very useful. A major feature is that it requires no setting up in the system it is to operate with, and is not affected by changing acoustic conditions.

This is especially advantageous with quick set-ups with which there is little time to make lengthy adjustments before going 'on the air'. All that is required is to connect it between the mixer and the amplifier and switch on. The internal adjustments should stay good for some time once they are made, although they may require re-setting once in a while.

Drawbacks

The 5 Hz shift has no audible effect on speech, but it does have on music. If the shift resulted in a small uniform change of pitch over the musical scale there would be no problem, but being a fixed frequency, the proportion changes. For example, middle C has a frequency of 261 Hz, and C# which is a semitone higher has a frequency of 276.5 Hz, a difference of 15.5 Hz. A 5 Hz shift is thus a third of a semitone sharp here.

At two octaves below, C_2, the frequency is 65.4 Hz and C# is 69 Hz, a difference of 3.6 Hz. Here, a 5 Hz shift is equivalent to well over a semitone. At C_3, there is only 4 Hz difference between C and D, so 5 Hz is more than a whole note sharp.

If music is played through a frequency-shifter, the result is quite inharmonious, and it sounds as though the bass players are playing all wrong notes. So groups, singers, or other live music performers would be well advised not to use a shifter!

The same effect is obtained with recorded music, but anti-feedback measures are not required for records so a frequency-shifter would not be used anyway. If a public-address system has provision for recorded music as well as speech, and a frequency-shifter is used, the tape or disc input should be designed to bypass the shifter.

This may not be easy as auxiliary inputs are usually controlled through a mixer, and the shifter is connected between the mixer and the power amplifier. One way around the problem would be to have a second output socket on the mixer and two paralleled input sockets on the amplifier. A single-pole double-throw switch on the control panel is wired to switch in either of the mixer output sockets.

The frequency-shifter is connected between one mixer socket and one amplifier input, while a screened lead connects the other two. The switch would then select either the shifter or the bypass lead, enabling the operator to switch out the shifter when music is played. Alternatively, a bypass switch could be fitted to the frequency-shifter itself thus saving the fitting of extra sockets, but the shifter would have to be placed in a convenient position near to the main control panel. No such problem exists with the variable notch filter as music is not degraded in any way; in fact, the opposite is true.

We have seen that a notch filter restores tonal balance by removing the peaks added by the system, and also reduces confusing reverberation which centres around those peaks. So as well as giving more gain before feedback, a notch filter cleans up the sound of speech and generally improves it.

This advantage is not obtained with a frequency-shifter. Its action could be said to skate over the peaks, thus preventing them causing feedback, but they remain to colour normal non-fedback signals, and reverberation is likewise not reduced.

A phase shift of exactly 90° at all frequencies may not be obtained, so the minus signals may not fully cancel. The result could be a beat between the two and amplitude modulation. Although this is likely to be only a small amount, it is a further degradation of the signal in addition to the disproportionate pitch changes over the frequency spectrum.

So, the frequency-shifter has its snags, but nonetheless is a very effective tool for reducing feedback, and is convenient in that it needs no setting up on site. However, it does not confer the same advantages as the variable-notch filter, and should not be used for acoustic musical instruments although it could have a role with electric guitars and percussion.

Chapter 7

GROUP MUSIC AND FEEDBACK

While much of what has been said before applies to live musical performances there are some special considerations. Electronic keyboard instruments have no vulnerability to feedback at all, as no sound-sensitive elements are involved. Microphones used for vocals or percussion could generate feedback, as also to a lesser extent, could the electronic stringed instruments.

Acoustics

The performance will possibly be given on a fairly large stage rather than a small platform, and it is likely to be for just a single occasion. In these circumstances fitting the rear wall with an absorbent is not very practical, and the performers will in most cases have to accept whatever acoustics they find. If the stage is that of a theatre, there should be no problem with damping, as there will be a back curtain as well as side curtains.

For non-amplified music such as orchestral, choral, chamber music or recitals, a theatre stage is the worst possible environment except the open air. For these, reverberation is essential to give volume and sonority to the sound, and even large, first-class orchestras sound thin and second-rate when playing in such venues.

On the other hand, concert halls designed to give the required reverberation to acoustic instruments, can produce feedback problems when amplification is used.

Direct Feedback

As with any p.a. system, direct feedback should be prevented by ensuring that main system loudspeakers are directed away from all microphones, which means stacking them on the stage forward from the microphones. Another possibility that has been mentioned before, is that of feedback through the structure of the stage from loudspeakers to microphones.

This can be prevented by mounting both on felt pads or fibreglass. If the latter is used it should be encased in fabric (a cushion case would do), to avoid it becoming a health hazard.

Foldback loudspeakers, that is those used to monitor the sound so that players can hear themselves, should be run at only sufficient volume to do just that. Furthermore, none should be right on-axis with a microphone.

Vocals

While in theory feedback is always possible with a microphone used for vocals, it is less likely with the close miking currently in vogue. This is because the ratio of direct sound from the vocalist to indirect feedback, is much greater than when the microphone is used at a normal distance. Thus the gain can be turned down, yet still be adequate.

This type of miking though, calls for a modification to what has previously be said about the type of microphone to be used. The cardioid and hypercardioid which are normally recommended, are very sensitive to explosive consonants which occur with close miking. These are the b and p sounds which blow the diaphragm violently forward with the velocity of escaping breath. As the diaphragm is open to the air on both sides there is no restraining cushion of air behind it.

A slight reduction of this effect can be obtained by using a 'pop' shield, that is a foam envelope over the end of the microphone, but its effect is only slight. A much larger and elaborate shield is needed to really avoid it.

In the case of an omni-directional microphone, the diaphragm works against a sealed chamber, it is pressure rather than velocity operated. So it responds less violently to the explosive consonants.

Another effect of pressure gradient microphones is that bass is exaggerated when the instrument is used on-axis in close proximity to the source. At 5-in (10 cm) the bass between 100 Hz and 50 Hz is boosted by some 6 dB. At 1-in (2 cm), the base is boosted by a further 6 dB approximately. This does not occur with an omni.

Vocalists who may have a rather thin-sounding voice may find a bass lift an advantage, and so could benefit from using a cardioid or hypercardioid. Others would prefer a more natural sound and also to avoid the p and b problems, so would find an omni better.

However, as pointed out in Chapter 4, omnis are more prone to feedback, yet with close miking the effect is reduced. So, while the choice is broadly between natural tone and reduced feedback, personal preference will play a large part.

Should feedback prove a problem with an omni microphone, a notch-filter could be used to eliminate resonance peaks and so reduce it. As the frequency range of pop vocalists does not descend into the bass register, a frequency-shifter could be used as an alternative. The 5 Hz shift should not unduly affect the pitch, and the feature of instant use with no setting up could be an advantage.

Percussion Microphones

These are further from the source than vocal units, so could be more liable to feedback. If one or two microphones are covering a number of percussion instruments, a fairly wide polar response will be required. In this case the cardioid would be the best choice. This has quite a wide acceptance angle, yet rejects rear sound. Thus feedback is reduced without unduly curtailing the frontal pickup. A hypercardioid would have too narrow a response unless used only for one percussion unit.

Here too a frequency-shifter could be used, as apart from the tympani, percussion has only random pitch. So although low frequencies are generated, there would be no inconvenient pitch change.

Strings

Electronic stringed instruments such as the guitar, can give rise to feedback if sound from the loudspeakers impinges on the strings. As with microphones they should be played behind the loudspeaker stacks.

Feedback is more likely to occur as a result of sympathetic vibration of the open unstopped strings. While one or two may be more prone than the others, any could initiate feedback when played hard. A notch-filter would thus have to be tuned to each of the strings to reduce the possibility. As there are six of these, that makes a formidable filter unit. Furthermore, the filter could rob those strings of their impact by reducing their volume while affecting surrounding notes to a lesser amount.

The alternative is the frequency-shifter, yet as we have seen, it sharpens the bass register. This makes it unusable for acoustic instruments, but not necessarily for electronic ones.

The way round the problem is simply to tune the guitar with the frequency-shifter operating. The instrument will actually be slightly flat in the lower strings, but as there is no acoustic output, it will sound in tune over its whole range through the system, which is what matters. With amplified acoustic guitars this would not be so, and a frequency-shifter could not be used.

So, if a single mixer and amplifier system is used, one frequency-shifter could be used for all inputs which could greatly simplify the set-up.

It can be seen then, that group feedback problems need somewhat different treatment from that employed with speech reinforcement systems due to special considerations.

Chapter 8

HOW *NOT* TO CURE FEEDBACK

No, that is not a mis-print. In this chapter we are going to look at a few feedback 'cures' that do NOT work. This is not as pointless as it may seem but has a practical purpose.

Feedback being the universal problem it is, has exercised the minds of most p.a. operators ever since someone set up the first microphone/amplifier/loudspeaker system to reinforce speech. Many have dreamed of finding the p.a. operator's philosopher's stone, the perfect cure in which feedback is totally eliminated. Like the philosopher's stone, it has remained a dream. Many ideas have been evolved, some hopeless from the start, others which seemed to hold out promise in theory, but which did not work in practice.

By taking a look at some of these, much time and effort can be saved for anyone who may have similar ideas, and disappointments avoided.

Signal Interruptor

This idea depended on the fact that feedback needs a continuous signal to keep the oscillation going. If a fader is turned down for example, the feedback ceases. It is also true that very small signal interruptions pass unnoticed by most listeners. So, the theory was that if a small interruption of a few milliseconds is introduced, during which there is a complete cessation of the signal, the feedback cycle is broken and feedback ceases or is not allowed to build up. The signal is resumed for a few more milliseconds, then broken again and so on.

A prototype interruptor was built using a multivibrator to generate a square wave. This shorted the input of one of the amplifying stages at one half-cycle, and removed the short at the next. The frequency of the multivibrator was made adjustable and also the mark/space ratio, which is the ratio between the two half-cycles of the square wave. There was thus plenty of flexibility to try different timings for the interruptions and the 'on' periods.

Electronically, the interruptor worked perfectly and timings could be varied over a wide range. One problem that immediately became apparent was a buzz that was produced by the switching transients. This could probably have been cured, but there was little point in trying because the device was found to have virtually no effect on feedback.

The reason was that if the 'on' periods were long enough to give the audible effect of continuous uninterrupted sound and the interruptions short enough not to be noticed, they were long and short enough respectively to establish and sustain feedback.

Capacitor Isolator

Another idea developed by a colleague, was based on the principle that feedback occurs because a microphone and loudspeaker are operating with amplification in the same air volume at the same time. So according to the theory, if the microphone was on when the loudspeaker was off and vice-versa, feedback would not occur.

A circuit was devised in which the input signal was sampled, and the samples stored in a capacitor, which then discharged into the input circuit of the power amplifier. This took place rapidly, and the conditions were thus satisfied that the loudspeaker was producing the sound only at the instant the microphone was dead.

The circuit was built and worked as designed — but it did not reduce feedback. The reason in this case was that the reverberation of the auditorium was feeding sound to the microphone when the loudspeaker was off, it behaved as a sound reservoir, so maintaining the feedback signal and the coupling.

Noise Gate

This is a useful device for eliminating noise during periods when there is no wanted signal. One use is the playing and re-recording of old 78 records that have high noise levels between tracks and gaps in the recorded sound. A noise gate cuts it completely. Although it has no effect on the noise during the recorded part of the record, this is masked to a great extent by the music itself. At the instant the music ends the gate switches off so silencing the noisy run-out grooves.

It works by switching on only for signals above a predetermined level which is set just above noise level. It thus remains off until a signal arrives that exceeds the preset level. Response can be very rapid so that none of the wanted signal is lost when it switches on. Once on it stays on until the signal again drops below the specified level, when it again switches off.

As feedback starts at a small level, it seemed that a noise gate might prevent it starting. A gate was rigged to an amplifier, with near miraculous results; the gain could be turned full up with the microphone directly pointing at the loudspeaker and not a hint of feedback!

Unfortunately as soon as someone attempted to speak into the microphone, the full violence of feedback was unleashed, as of course the signal switched the gate off. So it works as long as no-one uses the microphone — not a very practical arrangement! This was really expected from the start, but it was worth a try.

Delayed Sound

Another avenue that seemed promising was delaying the sound from the loudspeakers. It was thought that this might inhibit the build-up of feedback because there would be no immediate reinforcement of the original trigger sound. Furthermore the delay should reduce the frequency of oscillation if it did occur. With a long enough delay, the feedback frequency could be below the bass response of the system.

A delay line using a bucket-brigade chip and variable delay control was tried, but there was no reduction in feedback. It might have delayed the start by a small amount, but once initiated, a continuous oscillation at the feedback frequency was maintained. The delay merely meant that the microphone was picking up previous cycles of oscillation to reinforce the present ones.

To test the idea to an extreme, a much longer delay of about one second was tried using a closed tape loop. Feedback still occurred, but it proceeded in a series of bleeps. Even if it had been effective, such a delay would have been obvious and unacceptable to an audience, as well as being difficult for a speaker to speak against a continual echo.

One interesting effect was noticed though with the variable delay line. If the delay time was slowly increased, feedback disappeared as long as the increase continued. As soon as the increase stopped when the control reached maximum, feedback recommenced. Another effect noted was that the pitch of the reproduced sound was lowered during the delay increase. This too returned to normal when the increase ceased.

It is obviously impractical to continue increasing the delay indefinitely beyond a small fraction of a second, so although it does work as a feedback filter, the principle of continual delay is unusable as it stands. A possible way around this would be to modulate the delay line with a saw-tooth waveform so that there is a gradual increase in delay followed by a quick return to zero delay to start another increase.

Each return would mean a loss of that part of the signal that had been delayed. Also the system would have to be muted during the flyback otherwise the pitch of the reproduced sound would rise momentarily just as with a tape fast forward. It seems doubtful that these events would pass unnoticed, but it is not impossible that with a short delay run and a fast flyback, an acceptable solution could be found.

Out-of-phase Microphones

This idea is based on the principle of the noise-cancelling microphone. These are used for announcing in noisy locations and they consist of a hand-set containing two transducers which are separated by a few inches, and connected out-of-phase with each other.

The announcer speaks into one transducer and although the speech is also picked up by the other, the closer proximity of the first produces a larger signal. So cancellation is only partial, and a signal output is obtained. The noise source being further afield, is more or less equidistant from both transducers, and so affects both equally. Cancellation of noise is therefore almost total. The ratio between speech and noise is thereby greatly increased.

At high frequencies the speech signal is actually reinforced when the spacing between the transducers is greater than half a wavelength. Then, the acoustic wave is out-of-phase, but reinforcement occurs because the transducers are connected out-of-phase. Low frequencies arrive at the two transducers in phase and so are cancelled.

The effect is that having no low frequencies, the sound is rather tinny. This is not a major drawback where spot announcements are involved, but would be unacceptable for a good quality p.a. system, as would the necessity of the speaker having to hold the microphone close to the mouth. So the use of noise-cancelling microphones to avoid feedback, although workable, is not desirable.

The idea has been tried of using this principle in modified form. It involves having another microphone on stage a few feet away from the one being used, and connected in opposite phase. In theory the reflected signal from the auditorium should generate an anti-phase signal in the microphone which can be balanced out with the mixer fader leaving only the wanted signal from the programme microphone.

In practice while there is some cancellation, the effect on feedback is limited. The reason is that although they sound the same, the reflected signals arriving at one point on the stage are different in phase and comparative strengths from those just a few feet away. Low frequencies are similar, but all those having wavelengths shorter than the distance between the microphones will have phase and level differences.

Cancellation becomes greater as the microphones are moved closer together and there is a closer correspondence between the sound fields received by each. Finally, if the instruments are well matched, almost complete cancellation occurs when they are side-by-side. The snag is that the wanted signal is also affected, and as the microphones become closer, the bass is progressively reduced producing a very tinny result, until the signal disappears altogether.

If a very strong reflection is coming from the back of the hall but very little from the sides, an out-of-phase microphone could give a worthwhile reduction of feedback. This is because in this situation the wavefront is almost a plane wave and it reaches both microphones in phase at all frequencies. In most cases the ambience consists of random reflections from many different angles which is why the sound field can differ so markedly between two fairly close points.

Gun Microphone

These are often seen in outdoor t.v. news films, as a long barrel that is pointed toward the subject. Their feature is that they have a very narrow forward acceptance angle being insensitive to sounds coming from the side and back, over the frequency range of the instrument.

The principle is quite a simple one, a tube having a series of holes drilled along one side is mounted in front of the diaphragm. Sound pressure waves coming from the side enter the tube at the free end and also at the side holes, but the length of each path to the diaphragm varies according to the location of the hole. From the first hole it is the shortest, while from the end of the tube it is the longest.

The resulting series of delays produce cancellation hence zero pick-up from side-arriving sounds. Feedback can thereby in theory be reduced. When the pressure wave arrives from the front, the paths through the tube-end and all holes are equal, so reinforcement takes place.

Rejection of side waves is dependant on frequency and also the length of the tube. It is greatest at highest frequencies and for the longest tubes. A 24-inch tube is effective above 100 Hz and gives about 10 dB rejection. We saw in Chapter 4 that the cardioid microphone could be placed at 1.7 times the distance from the source for the same pick-up of indirect sound, and a hypercardioid twice the distance. A 24-inch gun will give the same results at around 3.5 times the distance. A smaller tube of 8½ inches is effective only down to 1 kHz and can operate at about 2.75 times the distance.

Below the effective operating frequency, the device behaves as it would without the tube. This is an important factor. If the basic microphone is a hypercardioid, it will behave as such in the lower register, but if it is an omni it behaves as an omni.

While some improvement may be gained by fitting a short tube to a hypercardioid, if the transducer is an omni, any benefit afforded by the tube is nullified. The microphone also needs to have a flat response. Some short-tubed commercial microphones use omnis and are actually worse than a good hypercardioid for reducing feedback. Omnis can be identified by the lack of vents in the capsule behind the diaphragm.

A 24-inch tube is too directional for public-address, the speaker needs only to turn his head and the sound fades. It is also very unwieldy. The 8½-inch tube is more practical, but needs to be fitted to a hypercardioid with a flat response. It too is rather over-directional and could result in fading as the speaker moves. As major system peaks appear below 1 kHz, these would be unaffected by the tube.

Although some benefit may result from a good short-tubed gun microphone, there are pitfalls, and in general they are not recommended.

So there they are, a collection of ideas that didn't work; perhaps they will save some reader a lot of fruitless effort in going over the same ground again. The only measures that have been found to be successful in improving the feedback characteristics of an already well-designed system are the frequency-shifter and the variable-notch filter.

Not that technology will never come up with the philosopher's stone one day. A possibility lies in the widening field of digital audio. The input signal could be converted to digital with an analogue/digital converter as contained in every CD player, then submitted to a microprocessor that could identify a rapidly repeated signal which would be the feedback. This could be digitally filtered out leaving only the original which would then be applied to a digital/analogue converter.

The resulting output would be pure distinct signal without any feedback or reverberation. It sounds complicated but far more complicated things are done in every CD player and digital recorder.

Chapter 9

DEALING WITH INSTABILITY

Instability is akin to acoustic feedback in that it consists of unwanted signals being fed back to an earlier point in the amplification chain. In this case the signals are electrical rather than sound, and tracing their path and cause can be one of the most difficult tasks to face the public-address engineer.

Like acoustic feedback, when part of the output signal finds its way back to an earlier stage, it passes again through the amplifier, arrives back at the output further amplified, is fed back again to the input point, is amplified even more, and so on. It rapidly builds up to a hoot or whistle.

Sometimes the instability can be supersonic and inaudible, but it can drive the amplifier to full power and so causes distortion of the wanted signal. It can also cause overheating and possible damage to the output transistors if allowed to continue. Often, cases of distortion are found to be due to high frequency instability. Although the loudspeakers may not reproduce it, it can usually be detected by means of the amplifier output meter which shows full output without any audible signal. Sometimes the meter needle is hard over against its end stop, in which case switch off immediately!

Types of Coupling

There are three types of coupling that can produce instability: *capacitive*, *magnetic*, and *common impedance*. Capacitance can exist between any components or leads, and any others that are in close proximity to them. Capacitors conduct alternating currents, so stray capacitances can likewise conduct a signal current between two leads or components. The amount of capacitance is proportional to their facing area and inversely proportional to the spacing between them.

Capacitors offer an impedance to the alternating currents that they conduct, the impedance, or more strictly the reactance, increases as the capacitance decreases. Furthermore, the reactance is frequency dependent, it is highest at low frequencies and diminishes as frequency increases.

Usually, stray capacitance around the amplifier and its wiring is not very great, so coupling at audio frequencies is insignificant. Thus audible instability due to stray capacitance is uncommon, but it can occur at supersonic frequencies. A general rule of thumb is that if instability can be heard it is unlikely to be due to capacitive coupling. To eliminate high frequency instability, many public-address amplifiers have a capacitor across their output to bypass high frequencies.

Electromagnetic coupling is a more likely cause. All cables carrying current have a magnetic field around them consisting of concentric lines of force which expand and contract as the current varies. If a cable carrying a large signal current runs parallel with another, the varying magnetic field will induce sympathetic currents into it. So loudspeaker feeders must be kept well away from microphone cables even though the latter are screened. Screening reduces the field penetrating to the conductor within, but does not block it completely.

If speaker and microphone cables have to cross they should do so at right angles, and never should they be run together. Likewise leads to tape decks or other auxiliary inputs should be physically separate from output leads.

Diagnosis is simply a case of turning all the faders down. If the instability disappears, there is a coupling between one of the inputs and the output circuits. Fading each up in turn should identify which input is at fault when the instability returns.

If turning down the faders has no effect and the instability persists, it is not due to capacitive or magnetic coupling between input circuits and output. The remaining type of coupling is common impedance.

Common Impedance Coupling

This occurs when an impedance is common to both input and output circuits. A common example is when the non-earthed side of a speaker feeder develops a leak to earth. There is then a path from one side of the output transformer secondary to earth, and from the other side through the amplifier, and the screened lead to the mixer, to earth. Part of the output signal is thus travelling along the braid of the mixer lead together

Fig. 20. An earth leak from a non-earthed loudspeaker feeder can complete a path from the output transformer to the mixer earth connection via the screen of the mixer lead. The screen resistance and inductance form a common impedance with mixer output signal. The inductance offers a higher impedance hence coupling, to high frequencies. Oscillation frequency is therefore high, possibly supersonic and may be heard as distortion due to amplifier overloading.

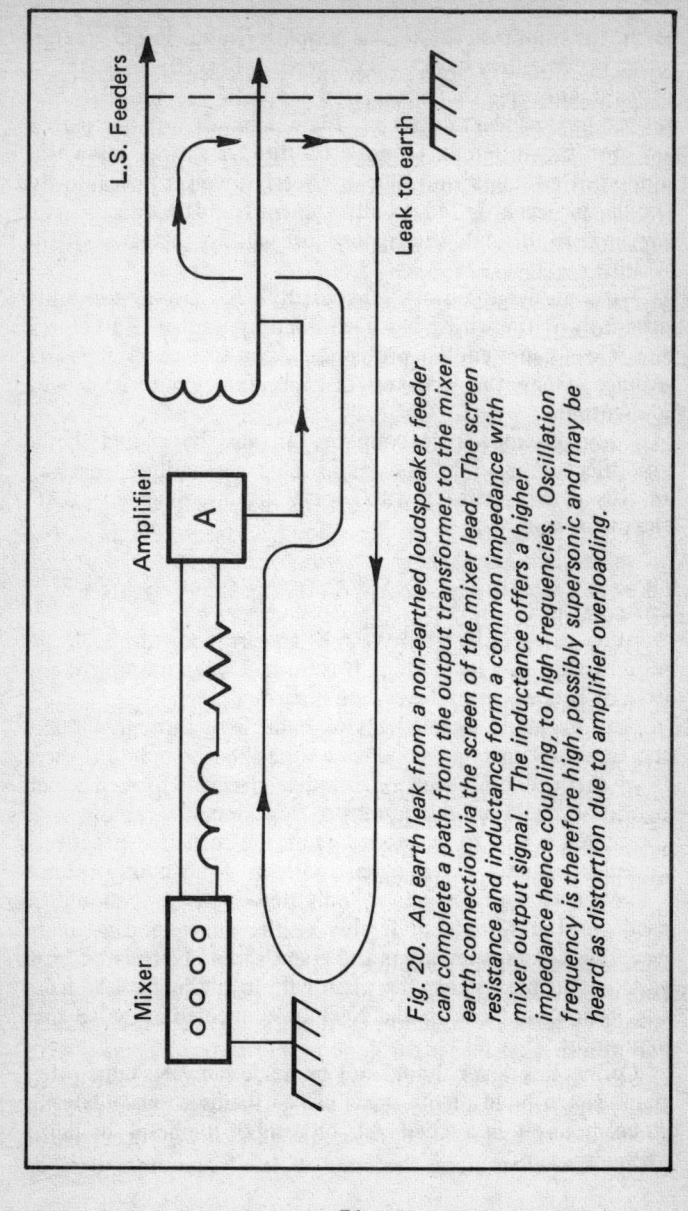

with the input signal to the amplifier, and coupling takes place because they have a common path (Fig. 20).

Disconnecting the mixer lead stops it, yet turning down all the mixer faders does not. If a number of amplifiers are in use feeding different sections of the system, all show the symptom although only one is directly involved, because the oscillation signal is fed to all of them from the mixer. This makes it so difficult to diagnose just what is the cause of the trouble.

With all large installations earth leaks are a possibility especially if the wiring has been done by unqualified helpers; and it can cause endless problems. A routine check for earth leakage from the speaker distribution circuit is a wise precaution.

Common impedance coupling can also be caused in the amplifier or mixer by the failure of a decoupling capacitor. In this case it persists with everything disconnected except the mains supply.

Earth Loop

Another cause of instability can be an earth loop although this more usually results in hum. It is formed when more than one item of equipment in the system is earthed.

Any magnetic signal fields or hum fields through which a screened cable may pass, induce a voltage in the braid. If there is an earth at both ends, a complete circuit is formed which permits a signal or hum current to flow along the braiding. As the screen is part of an input circuit, the current is effectively in series with the input signal and hum or instability results.

To prevent an earth loop, only one earth point should be used for the system, preferably to the mixer, and auxiliary items such as tape recorders and grams should be isolated from earth. This means that the earth wire in the mains lead from any item except one should NOT be connected in the 13-amp mains plug.

Connecting links should not be made between units other than via the braid of the signal cable. If this is unavoidable as when mounted in a metal rack, one end of the braid should be open circuit.

A loop can be formed when tape-in and tape-out leads are taken from a tape recorder to a mixer to afford record and play facilities. In such a case only one braid should be continuous, the other being connected at one end only. If both are continuous, hum or instability can result.

Chapter 10

BUILDING THE VARIABLE-NOTCH FILTER

As we have seen in earlier chapters, a variable-notch filter reduces feedback by eliminating the major resonance peaks in the system that trigger feedback, and thereby allows the gain to be raised to near feedback level. Unlike the graphic equalizer it tunes exactly to the frequency of the peak. In addition, it reduces amplified reverberation around the frequencies of the peaks and thereby considerably improves clarity. The unit here described is a twin-notch filter which enables two peaks to be eliminated.

As the first peak to appear is bound to be the largest, and the second to appear, the second largest, it follows that the two largest peaks are thereby removed. Extra filters could be added to remove third and fourth peaks and more, but we then enter the province of diminishing returns. Each peak is smaller than the last, so notching those out after the first two brings little extra gain. Some systems get excellent results with only one notch.

Specification

The device has an overall gain of 18 dB which can be useful, and means that the extra head-room can be fully utilized. It may be possible to use boundary or pressure-zone microphones as a result of the improved feedback characteristic, and as these are used at a distance, more gain is needed for them.

An input of 100 mV is the maximum otherwise the filter will start clipping the signal waveform and introduce distortion. If the mixer has an output meter the level can be adjusted accordingly. If not, check what the maker's specified output is and if higher, keep the faders down.

The notch at maximum depth takes out −18 dB which should remove any peak ever likely to be entered. The frequency range of the notch is 30 Hz to 8 kHz continuously variable, which well covers the frequencies over which peaks normally appear.

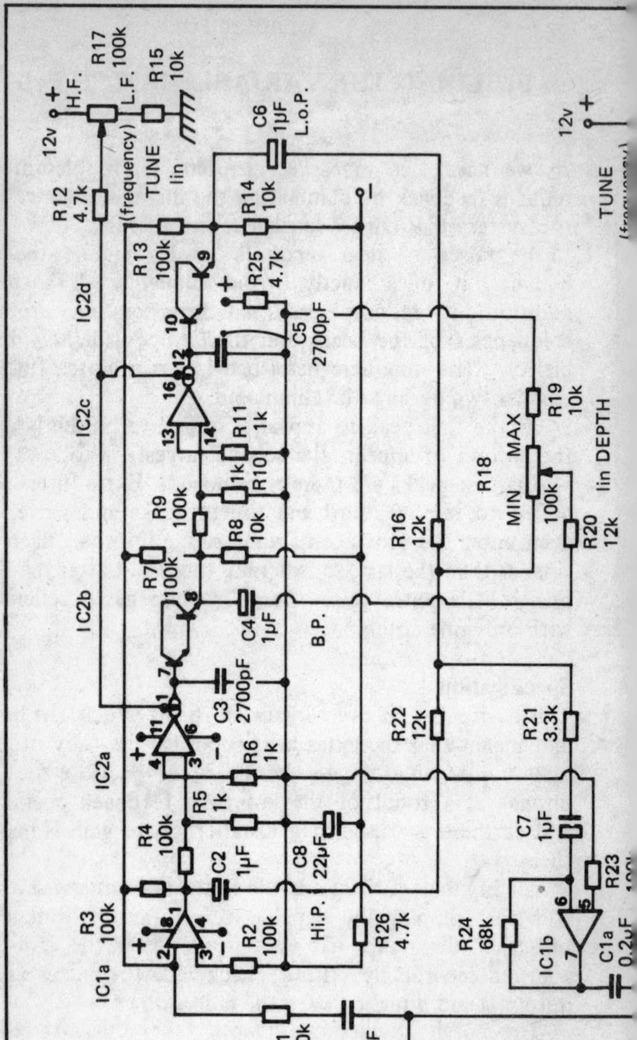

12v
H.F.
R17 100k
L.F.
R15 10k
(frequency)
TUNE
lin
C6 1μF
L.o.P.
R12 4.7k
R14 10k
R13 100k
R25 4.7k
C5 2700pF
IC2d
IC2c
R11 1k
R10 1k
R9 100k
R8 10k
R7 100k
R16 12k
R18
MIN MAX
100k
lin DEPTH
R19 10k
R20 12k
IC2b
C4 1μF
B.P.
C3 2700pF
IC2a
R6 1k
R5 1k
R22 12k
R21 3.3k
C7 1μF
R4 100k
C2 1μF
C8 22μF
R3 100k
R2 100k
Hi.P.
R26 4.7k
R24 68k
IC1b
R23
C1a
IC1a
R1 100k
C1 0.2uF
IN
TUNE

Fig. 21. Variable-Notch Filter Circuit Diagram.

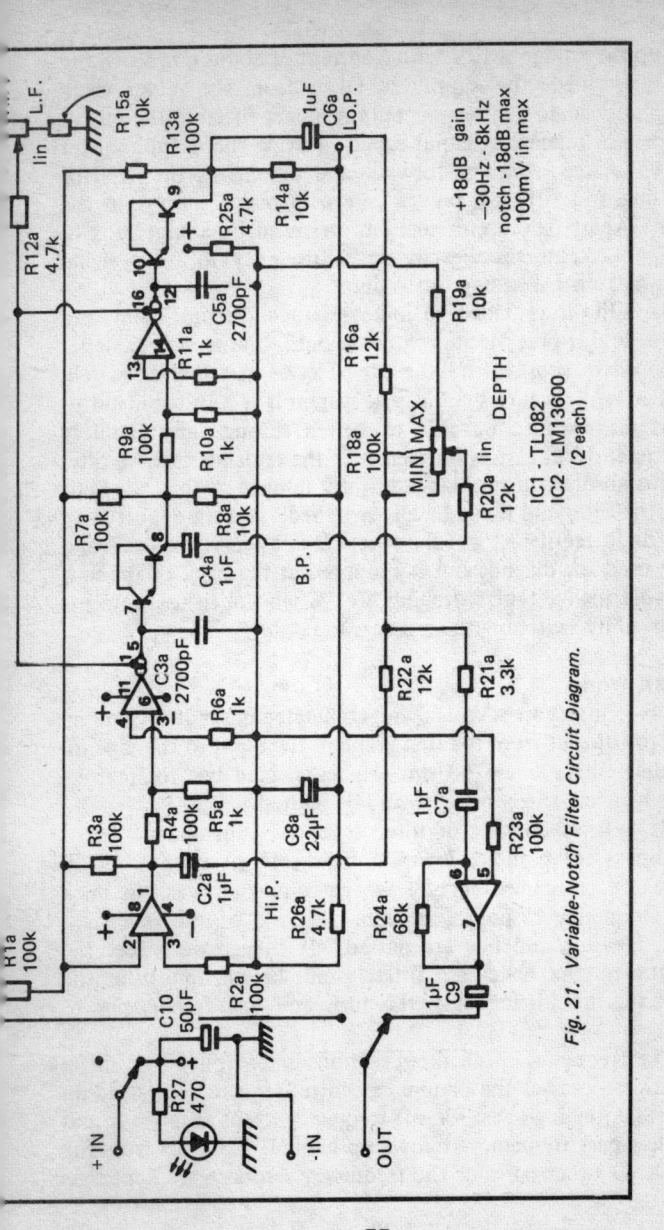

Supply voltage is 12V with a current of about 6 mA. In the unit described, the supply is taken from the mixer via a screened lead to a three-pin output socket fitted to the mixer, which also carries the input signal. Fitting the output socket to the mixer is straightforward and eliminates the need of building and fitting a power unit with mains supply, in the filter. Apart from extra cost and the need for a larger box to house it, mains supplies in close proximity to audio signal units make them vulnerable to hum.

An LED is provided to indicate when the unit is on, and also a double-pole, double-throw switch. One section switches the positive supply, and the other serves as a bypass switch.

If a fault occurs on the p.a. system it is a valuable aid to rapid diagnosis to be able to switch through any ancillary equipment that carries the signal. If the fault persists the filter is thus absolved from blame, but if it disappears then the fault is in the filter and it can be left switched out until opportunity affords to rectify it. As the switch is left permanently on and only used for diagnosis, it is mounted at the back of the unit to avoid inadvertent switching off. When not in use power is removed by switching the mixer off.

How it Works

The two filters are identical and connected in tandem (see Fig. 21), the output from the first going to the input of the second. Further filters could be similarly connected but for reasons already given, the benefits would be limited.

Each filter consists of three sections, a high-pass filter, a band-pass filter and a low-pass filter. If the outputs of all three are combined equally we get out what was put in, a flat frequency response, because all parts of the spectrum, high, medium and low are passed. If though we reduce the output of the band-pass filter, a notch will appear in the response, permitting only the high and low frequencies to pass.

The frequency of all three sections is controlled by a single control so that as the band-pass centre frequency is moved up the scale, the high-pass roll-off frequency keeps ahead of it, and the low-pass frequency follows up behind. So apart from the notch all other parts of the frequency response are kept flat.

Component Values for Figure 21

Resistors

R1	100k
R2	100k
R3	100k
R4	100k
R5	1k
R6	1k
R7	100k
R8	10k
R9	100k
R10	1k
R11	1k
R12	4.7k
R13	100k
R14	10k
R15	10k
R16	12k
R17	100k pot lin
R18	100k pot lin
R19	10k
R20	12k
R21	3.3k
R22	12k
R23	100k
R24	68k
R25	4.7k
R26	4.7k
R27	470R

Capacitors

C1	0.2
C2	1.0
C3	2,700 pF
C4	1.0
C5	2,700 pF
C6	1.0
C7	1.0
C8	22.0

| C9 | 1.0 |
| C10 | 50.0 |

All capacitor values are µF except C3 and C5, 16 V.D.C. or higher.

Semiconductors

| IC1 | TL082 |
| IC2 | LM 13600 |

Two each of most of the above components are required, the second having a suffix 'a' in the diagram.

By a process of signal current feedback the three filter characteristics are obtained with only two tuned circuits, which are formed by the capacitors C3 and C5, and the resistor network R12, R15 and the frequency control. The two capacitors should be close tolerance or selected on a bridge to give a close match.

The high-pass output is taken from the output of IC1a via C2, the band-pass output from the output of IC2b via C4, and the low-pass output from the output of IC2d via C6. All three are combined through buffer resistors R22, R16 and R20, but the latter from the band-pass filter, is taken through a potentiometer which functions as the depth control. When at minimum, all outputs are equal and the response is flat, but as the control is turned toward maximum, the output of the band-pass filter is reduced so forming the notch of increasing depth.

The notch has a roll-off of 6 dB per octave on either side which corresponds with that of most system peaks, but its bottom groove is sharp so that it can be aurally tuned spot-on to the peak. IC1b is the output buffer that also provides the gain.

Although the circuit may appear complex, most of it is contained within the two ICs, and construction is quite straightforward.

Construction

The filters are built separately on two identical matrix boards (see Figs 22 and 23), each of 19 strips and 29 holes. Extra length is required to accommodate the fixing holes at each end

Fig. 22. *Matrix Board Component Side.*

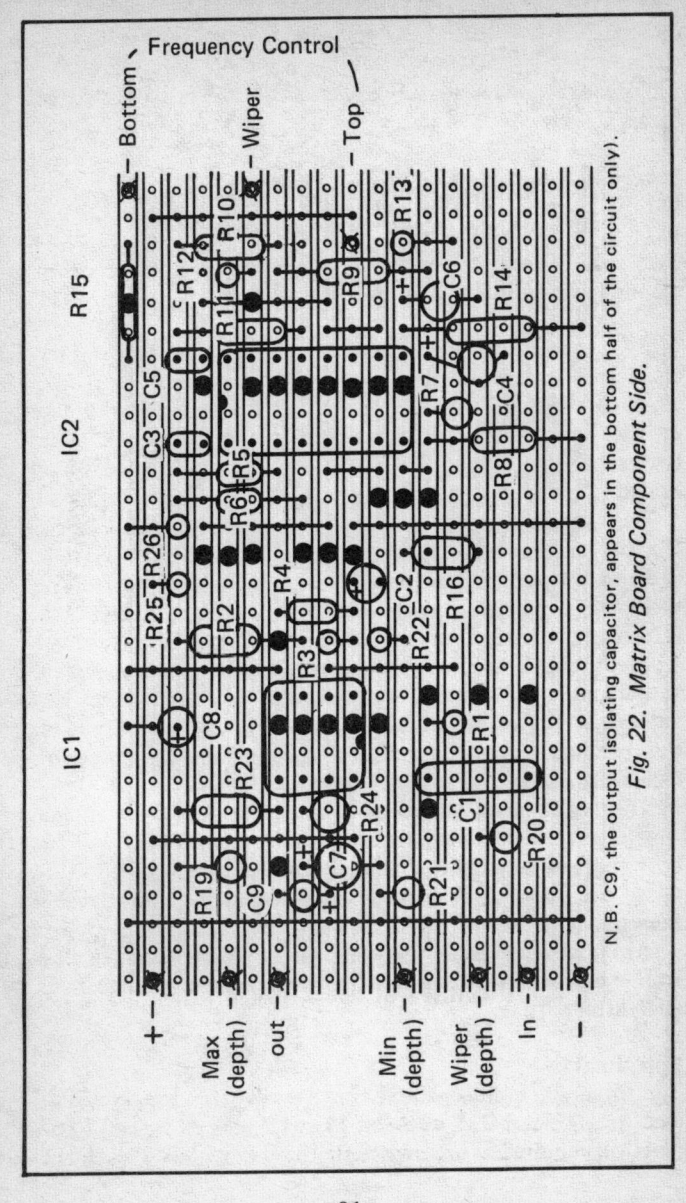

N.B. C9, the output isolating capacitor, appears in the bottom half of the circuit only).

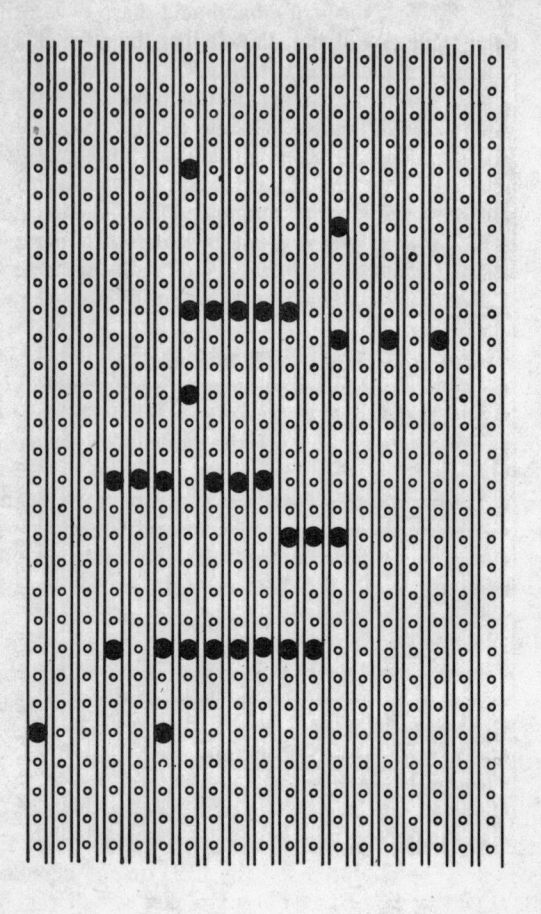

Fig. 23. Matrix Board Print Side.

but these are not shown on the plans.

The first step after drilling the fixing holes is to cut the conductors at the designated points as shown in the print-side plan. A special cutting tool is available for this or they can be cut with a few turns of a hand-held sharp twist drill of larger diameter than the strips. Ensure that the print is totally cut and no whiskers of copper are left.

Now fit the terminal posts which just press into the holes and are soldered, then the wire links as shown. Next, the IC holders can be soldered in place. It is nearly always better to use holders than solder the ICs in direct. The possibility of damage from heat is thereby eliminated as the ICs can be plugged in as the final step when all soldering is complete, and they can be easily changed if a faulty one is suspected. Make sure that the holders have their cut-outs at the ends shown.

The resistors and capacitors can now be inserted and soldered in. Double check the number of holes horizontally and vertically before soldering, errors are easy to make but not so easy to spot later. Ensure the polarity of electrolytic capacitors are correct.

When soldering is complete it always pays to examine the print, scanning each strip with a magnifying glass. It is surprising the tiny slivers of solder that can encroach on to the adjacent strip, also joints that looked sound when made but are seen to be anything but under magnification. Time spent at this stage can save a lot later.

Finally, insert the ICs. If the pins are splayed out, bend them to be vertical by heeling them one side at a time against a flat surface. When inserting, check that the dot is at the same end as the cut-out on the holder, and that all the pins actually go into the holder.

The case can be any metal box of convenient size. Metal is preferred to plastic because of the screening it offers. Four controls have to be mounted and the LED on the detachable front panel. The switch, an output socket which can be a phono or a jack, and the three-pin input socket must be fitted to the back of the box.

The layout of the prototype is shown in Figure 24, but any convenient layout can be chosen, others have been used

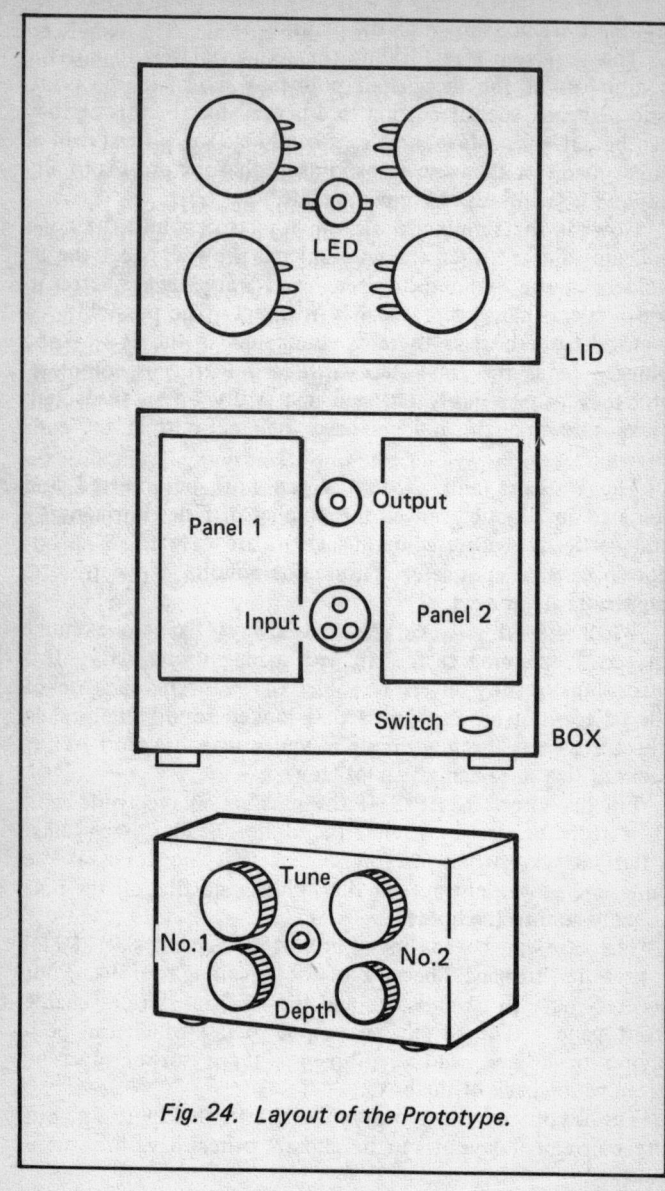

Fig. 24. Layout of the Prototype.

and it does not seem to be at all critical. The panels are mounted into the box ensuring any metal fixing does not contact the print. Nylon screws and nuts or supports prevent this possibility.

Wiring to the controls and sockets can now be done. When looking at the back of a control with the tags uppermost, the left-hand tag is the low or minimum one. C10 can be wired directly to the switch, or one of the positive terminal posts, whichever is the most convenient. Also R27 can be self-supported, wired to the LED or the switch. A lead must be taken from the output terminal of the first filter to the input of the second. If the gain is too great and overloading is a problem, it can be reduced by using a resistor for the link. The value will have to be by trial and error to obtain the desired gain.

Now the leads can be made up. Use twin screened for the input, one wire for the signal and the other for the positive supply. A single screened cable serves for the output lead. The screens go to chassis.

After fitting suitable knobs and labelling, the filter is ready for use.

Chapter 11

USING THE NOTCH FILTER

The unit is connected between the mixer and the power amplifier. Setting it up is quite straightforward and takes longer to describe than to do. First, turn all the controls anti-clockwise to their minimum position. Then advance the depth control of the No. 1 filter to about a third way up.

Now, with the microphone in its normal position turn up the main fader until feedback commences. Slowly turn the No. 1 tuning control clockwise until the feedback stops. You will find that you can tune right through it so that feedback recommences if you go any further. Find the centre of the peak by adjusting the knob slightly from side to side, just as you would tune in a radio station. The notch is now exactly on tune to the frequency of the first peak.

Next, turn the depth control back until feedback starts up again, then advance it until feedback just stops. Turn the microphone fader up until feedback recommences. If it is the same frequency as before, turn the depth control further. Chase the feedback by alternately turning up the fader and depth control until the feedback changes pitch.

This means that the first peak has been dealt with and the second peak has taken over. Repeat the above procedure using filter No. 2, tuning it to the peak with the depth control partly up, then adjusting the depth control and fader until feedback at that frequency stops.

After this one of two things may happen. Advancing the fader further may produce feedback at a third different frequency. If this happens, you have cleared the two main peaks and obtained a significant increase of gain before feedback. It is as far as you can go.

The other eventuality is that the first peak reappears. What has happened is that it was reduced to below the level of the second peak but not completely flattened. The second peak then took over, but when it in turn was taken down, what was left of the first peak regained prominence. Advancing the No. 1 depth control further will deepen the notch and reduce the peak to zero.

In turn this may cause the second peak to re-emerge for the same reason, in which case the No. 2 depth control should be advanced until this peak too disappears.

In some cases it may be found that when tuning out the first peak it disappears even when the tuning control is turned well past it, and another feedback frequency appears in its place. This happens when the two peaks are of similar height. One or the other may predominate, and a temporary loss of the one when it is tuned through, opens the way for the other to take over.

If this second one is notched out, the first one will re-appear. It can then be notched by filter No. 2. This is a desirable situation because eliminating two large peaks gives more extra gain than eliminating a large and a smaller one.

Short-cut Method

The procedure described gives a flat response over the area covered by the two main peaks, hence a natural-sounding reproduction. It takes very little time, certainly a lot less than setting up a graphic equalizer, and the time is further reduced when the operator has become familiar with the process.

An even quicker version is to turn the depth control up to about two-thirds and then tune out the first peak. The advanced depth control setting virtually ensures that there is nothing of the first peak left, so the chasing procedure with depth control and fader is avoided. The second peak is dealt with in the same way.

The only disadvantage of this quicker method, is that the depth of the notch will probably be greater than the height of the peak, so that the eventual response is not flat but has a residual notch. Feedback level is not thereby adversely affected and the aural effect is probably unnoticeable with speech, especially if the notch is not too deep.

Re-setting

It has been found that once set for any particular system, the filters rarely need re-setting. However, it may become necessary from time to time. Large temperature and barometric pressure changes affect the speed of sound, hence the wavelength of hall resonances; likely, loudspeaker and microphones could be affected too. Acoustics are also modified by the size of the audience. Ageing of components in the filter circuits could also have an effect.

The need for re-setting may become evident by a tendency to ring at the usual fader setting. In most cases all that is required is to rock the tuner controls slightly from one side to the other, one at a time, to tune out the ringing. If there is no improvement, increasing the notch depth a little by advancing the depth controls should do the trick. There is usually no need to go through the complete setting up procedure.

It is a good practice to use knobs with markers, and put a mark on the case with a felt pen to indicate the settings of all controls. Then if the knobs are inadvertently moved, perhaps by someone else, a glance at the markings will soon show it, and if they have been altered, they can be quickly corrected.

Tone Controls
Notch filters do not make conventional tone controls redundant. Beforehand they may have been used to try to reduce feedback, by for example, cutting the bass if the feedback was at a low frequency. When using filters, the tone controls should not be used for feedback control, but be set to the flat position before setting up.

Subsequently, the filters take over feedback suppression, and the tone controls can be used to balance the tone of the programme material. So, when hand-held directional microphones are used closer to the lips than usual, the resulting bass emphasis can be reduced by a little bass cut. Speakers with sibilant voices sound better with some treble cut, while those who have poor articulation can be rendered more intelligible with treble boost. When there is a large audience and the acoustics may be rather muffled, judicious treble boost will improve matters.

The operator should therefore listen continually to the tone quality of the programme to check what adjustments, if any, are required. Being liberated from the need to concentrate on feedback and getting enough gain, attention can be focused on the finer points of sound quality.

A final point of counsel. Always use a notch-filter, or frequency-shifter to improve on an already well-designed system following the guidelines described in earlier chapters. Never use it to paper over the cracks.

Index

A

Absorption of sound waves	21-24
Acoustic panelling	22
Acoustics and music	57
Air, springiness	5

B

Bar, unit of pressure	8

C

Capacitive coupling	69
Capacitor isolator	62
Cardioid response	38; 39; 58
Column loudspeaker	16-18
Comb-filter effect	12-13
Common impedance coupling	70
Curtaining	30-31

D

Decibel	8
Decibel ratios	9
Delayed sound	63
Diffraction of sound waves	19; 22; 24
Dipole	15-16
Direct feedback	57-58
Direct feedback path	27-29
Directivity	39
Doublet	15-16
Dyne	8

E

Earth loops	72
Electret microphone	36-37
Electromagnetic coupling	70
Explosive consonants	58

F

Feedback:	
direct	57-58
cause of	1-2
level	41
path	27-34
rate	2
Frequency	7
Frequency shifter	53-56; 59-60

G

Ghost images	19, 21
Graphic equalizers	48-49

Guitars and feedback	59-60
Gun microphone	66

H

Hertz	7
Human ear, volume control effect	9
Hypercardioid response	38; 58

I

Incipient feedback	41
Indirect feedback path	29-34
Instability	69
Interference	11

L

LISCA	13; 27
Line source	16-17
Loudspeakers:	
phasing	34
tilting	32-34

M

Membrane resonators	24
Microphones:	35-40
gun	66
cardioid	58
electret	36-37
hypercardioid	38; 58
moving coil	35
omnidirectional	58
percussion	59
ribbon	35-36
strings	59-60
supercardioid	38
vocalists	58-59
Monopole	13-15
Moving coil microphone	35

N

Newton	8
Noise gate	62
Notches:	
cancelling peaks	44
effect of displaced	46
effect of width	47

O

Octaves	48
Off-axis SPL	16
Omnidirectional response	37-38, 39; 58

O (continued)
Out-of-phase microphones — 64

P
Pascal — 8
Peaks:
    feedback level — 43
microphone — 44
Phase — 10
Pitch change with frequency shift — 54
Plane wavefront — 18
Platform rear wall covering — 30
Point source — 13-15
Polar response — 37-39
Presence effect — 35
Pressure gradient — 38; 39

Q
Quadrature — 10; 53

R
Reflection of sound waves — 19-21
Refraction of sound waves — 21
Resultants — 10-11
Reverberation:
    reduction with notch — 50
    time — 25
Ribbon microphone — 35-6

S
SPL:
    description — 8
    off-axis — 16

Signal interruptor — 61-62
Sound:
    absorption — 21-24
    attenuation with distance — 15
    diffraction — 19, 22
    intensity — 8
    pressure — 8
    reflection — 19
    refraction — 21
    speed of — 7
    transmission — 25
    wavefronts — 18
Sound waves — 5
Square law, sound propagation — 14-15
Supercardioid response — 38

T
Tone controls — 89

V
Variable notch filter:
    building — 75-85
    description — 50-51
    using — 87-90
Vectors — 11
Velocity microphone — 36; 38

W
Wavefronts — 18
Wavelength — 7